A COMMENTARY:
THE GOSPEL ACCORDING TO JOHN

DR. JOHN THOMAS WYLIE

authorHOUSE®

AuthorHouse™
1663 Liberty Drive
Bloomington, IN 47403
www.authorhouse.com
Phone: 1 (800) 839-8640

King James Version (KJV)
Public Domain

New International Version (NIV)
Holy Bible, New International Version˜, NIV˜ Copyright ©1973, 1978, 1984, 2011 by Biblica, Inc.˜ Used by permission. All rights reserved worldwide.

Revised Standard Version (RSV)
Revised Standard Version of the Bible, copyright © 1946, 1952, and 1971 the Division of Christian Education of the National Council of the Churches of Christ in the United States of America. Used by permission. All rights reserved.

Published by AuthorHouse 06/07/2017

ISBN: 978-1-5246-9608-5 (sc)
ISBN: 978-1-5246-9607-8 (e)

Print information available on the last page.

Any people depicted in stock imagery provided by Thinkstock are models, and such images are being used for illustrative purposes only. Certain stock imagery © Thinkstock.

This book is printed on acid-free paper.

CONTENTS

DEDICATION

This Intimate Gospel Of John is dedicated to my beloved brother and sisters. They are David W. Wylie, JoAnn McCree (Wylie), brother-n-law Jackie McCree,

Vanessya Fountain (Wylie) and in memory of my Late departed Sister, Charlotte Lavelle (Wylie) Dixon, And My Late Departed Mother, Sister Charlye Mae Wylie

Special Thanks And Dedication To Mother Clara Penny James Copeland, Zion Baptist Church, Mother Verelene F. Robinson, 14th Avenue Missionary Baptist Church Nashville, Tennessee

And

To Pastor Jimmy Terry Sr. And 1st Lady Servela Terry

And

The Tabernacle Baptist Church, Clarksville, Tennessee

"To God Be The Glory"
Reverend Dr. John Thomas Wylie

THE ABC'S OF JESUS

A – He is The Alpha And The Omega

B – He is The Beginning and The End

C – He is Christ – The Cricified Savior

D – He is Deliever Of Sinners

E – He is Everlasting And Eternal

F – He is Father Of The Faithful

G – He is God All By Himself, The Great Teacher

H – He is High And Holy

I – He is Israel's Great Deliverer

J – He is Just Jesus

K –He is King Of Kings

L – He is Lord of lords, He Is Love

M – He is Mary's Precious Baby

N – He is Nicodemus's Teacher

O – He is Omnipresent

P – He is The Prince Of Peace

Q – He is The Quickening Spirit

R – He is The Resurrection And Life

S – He is Savior And More Than Life To Me

T – He is Truth, Tried And Trusted

U – He is The Universal God

V – He is The Victim On Friday (But He Rose
   up on Sunday)

W – He is The Wade In The Water

X – He is Extraordinary

Y – My Yoke Is Easy, My Burdern Is Lightfoot

Z – He is Zealous, He Knows Your Zipcode, He Knows Just Where You Live

I Thank Mother Clara Penny-James Copeland (My God-Mother), Zion Baptist Church, Nashville, Tennessee For Her Contribution To This Great Book of Love!

Reverend Dr. John Thomas Wylie

INTRODUCTION

The Gospel Of John

The book is composed by the apostle and situated as the fourth book in the New Testament. It appears that the fundamental motivation behind the book is to show what genuine confidence in Jesus Christ is. Hence the thing "confidence" never happens. Then again the verb "to accept" is extremely visit.

John's point is that lone that confidence which is dynamic and working is supporting. Maybe his most grounded case is John 12:42, 43 where it is expressed that sure of the rulers put stock in Him yet would not admit Him.

The grandiose Jews had just verbal relationship to God as opposed to one which was living and working. Genuine confidence is that relationship to God which causes one to depend upon through trust and to submit by acquiescence to the will of God.

John The Apostle

The son of Zebedee and Salome (Mark 1:20;

Luke 5:10, Mark 15:40; Matt. 27:56). Jesus called John in the meantime with his sibling James and with Simon (Peter) and Andrew (Mark 1:19-20; Luke 5:10). Later John was been one of the twelve messengers (Mark 3:13-19). The books of the New Testament by and large authorize to his origin are: The Gospel According to John, I John, II John, III John, and the Book of Revelation.

The Date And Place Of Writing

As per Christian custom, John spent the last years of his life at Ephesus, where he carried on a service of lecturing and educating, and in addition composing. Starting here he was ousted (exiled) to Patmos in the rule of the Emperor Domitian.

His Gospel appears to presuppose an information of the Synoptic convention and therefore ought to be set toward the end in the arrangement, perhaps somewhere close to 80 and 90. Some have it even later. The revelation in Egypt of sections of the Gospel, which have been dated from the main portion of the second century, requires the written work of the Gospel inside the points of confinement of the principal century.

The Authorship

Despite the fact that the book does not name the author, he is demonstrated as the darling pupil' (21:20, 23, 24) and the nearby friend of Peter. The declaration of the antiquated church is such that this is John, the child of Zebedee (cf. 21:2). Irenaeus is the main witness.

A few researchers have addressed whether one who was unschooled and unpracticed (Acts 4:13) could have composed such a work. Time, inspiration, and the enablement of the Spirit should be under-assessed in assessing the capacity of John and the overcoming of impediment.

Numerous moderns like to hold that an obscure pupil is the genuine creator of this Gospel, despite the fact that the greater part of the material may well backpedal to John as its source. Be that as it may, this is an unnecessary trade of a known for an obscure (The Wycliff Bible Commentary, 1968).

Purpose Of The Book

On the positive side this is expressed in John 20:30, 31 as the trust that conviction will be made in the perusers that Jesus is the Christ, the Son of God, with the goal that life will come through confidence in him. The decision of material is computed to prompt to precisely this conclusion.

Subordinate destinations might be permitted, for example, the invalidation of Docetism, a perspective that precluded the genuine humaniaty from claiming Jesus (cf. 1:14), and the presentation of Judaism as an insufficient arrangement of religion that delegated its different sins by rejecting its guaranteed Messiah (1:11, etc)(The Wycliff Bible Commentary, 1968).

CHAPTER

ONE

Prologue
(1:1-18)

Immediately the writer shows the focal figure of the Gospel, however does not call him Jesus or Christ. Now he is the Logos (Word). This term has Old Testament roots, recommending there the ideas of astuteness, power, and an exceptional connection to God. It was generally utilized, as well, by scholars to express such thoughts as reason and intercession amongst God and the world.

In John's day all classes of perusers would have comprehended its reasonableness here, where disclosure is the keynote. Yet, the exceptional component is that the Logos is likewise the Son of the Father, who got to be distinctly incarnate keeping in mind the end goal to uncover God completely (1:14, 18).

In the preface we get to be distinctly mindful that John is keeping down in his utilization of the name Jesus Christ. (See likewise 1 John 1:1-4). Logos then turns into the first in a progression of spellbinding words that John will attract together this opening psalm. The question is: What does the word logos intend to the various perusers of the book, and why does John utilize it?

To the Jew the possibility of the Word of God is seen essentially as far as legitimate, inventive activity and creation happens, and furthermore in the prophets where, by the Word of God, his forceful will is made known to mankind.

For the Greeks who read this introduction, the word logos likewise has its own particular unique importance. "The stoics suspected that a heavenly rule of logos or reason is inside and behind the universe, and keeps up it in being and arrange" (Lightfoot, 1956).

See the delicate path in which John addresses that peruser who is socially Greek and who conveys to the introduction his or her own comprehension of logos as that feeling of reason or significance which arranges the entire of reality.

He has made utilization of the straightforward however significant word logos (word) which has a rich importance in both his own Jewish universe of experience and furthermore in the thoughtful custom of the Greeks. Seen then in the point of view of both customs, John is imparting the accompanying:

"Before all else was the discourse." "in the first place was meaning." Calvin draws together both these aims in his announcement: "With regards to the Evangelist calling the Son of God the Speech (The Word), the straightforward reason appears to me to be, to start with, in light of the fact that he is the unceasing astuteness and will of God; and also, on the grounds that he is the energetic picture of His motivation (Calvin, 1949).

By the recognizable proof of the logos with God to start with, John has obviously instructed the unceasing preexistence of Jesus Christ. He additionally settles the matter by the announcement, "all things were made through him."

Later in the Christian period Gnostic educators will deny this attestation, and will look to isolate the Redeemer from the Creator. They will show that a substandard divinity is in charge of the production of matter which for them then resolves the issue of wickedness on the planet.

However, the New Testament and the Old Testament will have nothing to do with such a precept. The world itself is made by the great choice of God.

John's psalm introduces the logos as individual. This is the drive of the pronoun deciphered "through him." The logos is not a status of reality, as in Buddhist religious contemplated ultimacy, or an awesome generic power, as in current religious power and completion developments.

The logos is PERSON. Presently we are at the radical focus of the attestation of the Bible. At the focal point of everything is the God of character who is in the profoundest sense "I Am." He is the person who represents himself. "In the feeling of Christian confidence, God is not to be found in the arrangement of divine beings. He is not to be found in the pantheon of human devotion and religious creative skill....I said that God is He who, as indicated by Holy Scriptures, exists, lives, and acts, and makes himself known" (Barth, 1958).

The Pre-existent Logos
(1:1,2)

The "start" of the Gospel (cf. Check 1:1) is tied in with the start of the creation (Gen. 1:1) and comes to past it to a look at the Godhead "before the world was" (cf. John 17:5). The Word did not get to be; he was. With God recommends fairness and in addition affiliation. The Word was God (divinity) without perplexity of the people.

The Cosmic Logos
(1:3-5)

He was the agent in creation. By him. Through him.

All things. grasp the totality of matter and presence, yet saw here in their individual status as opposed to as universe. Life is in him, not just through him. As the life, the Word conveyed light (the learning of God) to men. 5. The murkiness is essentially moral. Not everybody benefits by the light (cf. 3:19). Most likely the thinking is not indistinguishable with 1:9, 10; so the dimness grasped it not is a more improbable interpretation than the obscurity has not defeat it.

The Incarnate Logos
(1:6-18)

6. Was. Better, came. This is John's development ever, as sent from God. The

expression compresses the material of Luke 1:5-80; 3:1-6. 7. John sought witness or declaration, which is a main accentuation of this Gospel (1:15, 34; 5:33, 36, 37; 15:26, 27; 19:35; 21:24). His commission was to observer to the Light, which had been sparkling as far back as the Creation and was going to illuminate men with his nearness. The witness was intended to make men trust (the thing "confidence" does not happen in this Gospel, but rather the verb is right around an abstain; cf. 20:31).

9. The True Light does not make John a false light. It indicates light in the antitypical, extreme sense-the sun, not a flame. Subsequently, to worship John unduly after the Light has unfolded isn't right (3:30; Acts 19:1-7). The language structure of the verse in the Greek is troublesome.

The True light that edifies each man was appearing on the scene is the most plausible rendering. By his nearness among men the Logos would bring a brightening outperforming what he had been bearing men before his coming.

10, 11. The Light was genuine and shining, however the reaction was frustrating. Past this closeness in the two verses lie examined contrasts: was, came; the world, his own; knew not, got not. Inability to perceive the pre-incarnate Logos is more justifiable than the awful refusal of his own kin to get him when he came among them.

12, 13. Not all declined the Light. The individuals who got him picked up power (expert, appropriate) to wind up (without even a moment's pause) children (kids) of God. The individuals who got are depicted as the individuals who accept on his name (individual, See 20:31). These are two methods for saying a similar thing. Devotees are further portrayed as far as what God accomplishes for them.

They are born.... of God. This is not a characteristic procedure, for example, brings individuals into the world - not of blood (truly, bloods), proposing the blending of fatherly and maternal strains in multiplication.

The will of the tissue recommends the normal, human yearning for kids, as the will of man (the word for spouse) proposes the unique longing for offspring to bear on a family name. So the new birth, something heavenly, is painstakingly protected from perplexity with common birth.

14. Before confidence could realize the new birth, it needed to have a protest on which to rest, even the incarnation of the Word, the Son of God. God, having communicated in creation and history, where the movement of the Logos was apparent however his individual hidden, now uncovered himself through the Son in human frame, which was no negligible similarity, yet tissue.

John could have utilize "man" however he expressed reality of the incarnation determinedly in order to negate those with Gnostic inclinations. This bogus perspective of Christ declined to recognize that unadulterated god could take a material body, since matter was viewed as something insidiousness (cf. I John 4:2, 3; II John 7).

Abided. Tabernacled. In blend with greatness it proposes the customizing of the splendid cloud that refreshed on the sanctuary in the wild (Ex. 40:34). The Word incarnate is additionally the solution to Moses' petition (Exod. 33:18).

John has no record of the Transfiguration, for he introduces the entire service as a transfiguration, with the exception of that the light he talks about is good and otherworldly (brimming with effortlessness and truth - as opposed to something visual (cf. John 1:17).

15. Additionally see (cf. 1:7) is taken of the declaration of the Baptist in light of Jesus' open appearance. Jesus came after John in time however went before him in significance, even as He was before him as the Eternal One (cf. 1:1). 16. The Evangelist affirms the uniqueness of Christ.

John the Baptist as well as "all" devotees have shared of his fulness - the fulfillment of divinity (cf. full in a:14). Beauty for effortlessness pictures one indication of elegance as heaped on another - a completion without a doubt. 17. As Jesus Christ outperformed John (1:15), so does He exceed expectations Moses. Both brought something from God, however the one brought the law which censures, the other "beauty" which recovers from law. Truth recommends the truth of Christ's disclosure of God.

18. God is undetectable, being Spirit (cf. 4:24; I Tim. 6:16). Theophanies don't uncover his quintessence. Be that as it may, God's just Son (here the main compositions have God as opposed to Son; cf. John 1:1) does. In the chest (bosom) of the Father reviews with God (1:1).

The Son's main goal was to pronounce (the Greek word gives us our "exegete") the Father. Christ translated God to man. Nothing is lost (cf. Heb. 1:2, 3; Gal. 1:15).

The Testimony Of John The Baptist (1:19-36)

In his deep yearning to amplify Christ, John transformed a request about himself into a solid observer to the more prominent One going to show himself. Jesus' absolution on account of John, not described in this Gospel, had as of now happened (1:26).

19. The Jews. As common in John, this implies pioneers of the country. These ministers were of the Pharisees (v. 24). Two things incited the nomination: the solid proclaiming of John, which enraptured the hoards (Matt. 3:5), and his submersing action (John 1:26).

Such a man energized such a great amount of worry in these pioneers that they asked, Who workmanship thou? 20. John read their musings. They, similar to the hoards (Lk. 3:15), were thinking about whether he could be the guaranteed Christ.

21. His disavowal prompted to a moment address. Elias (Elijah) was normal before the happening to the Messiah (Mal. 4:5).

In spite of the fact that John was not Elijah face to face, he was that one in capacity (Matt. 17:10-13). By that prophet we are most likely to comprehend the prophet of Deut. 18:15, 18. By some he was taken to be unmistakable from the Messiah (John 7:40).

22-24. The delegation couldn't be happy with nullifications. Squeezed to uncover his part, John answered in the dialect of prescience (Isa. 40:3). It was a genuine recognizable proof. John had lived in the wild and there had lifted up his voice to report the close approach of the kingdom (Luke 1:80; 3:2, 3).

25-28. Such a minor part did not appear to be adequate support for John's organization of immersion (baptism). Be that as it may, he shielded himself - it was simply with water. It broadcasted the nearness of wrongdoing and the need of a filtration which he himself couldn't impact. A definitive work of decontamination (so he implied) rested with a more noteworthy than he, One who was still an obscure to the experts (1:26).

John numbered himself unworthy to be His hireling. This discussion was held at Bethabara, east of Jordan. Driving compositions have Bethany, not to be mistaken for the Bethany of 11:1, 18.

29. The following day presents another circumstance. The nomination had left and Jesus showed up on the scene. However there was no discussion between and John. Content with confirming to the Pharisees the significance of Christ, John now got to be distinctly particular about His individual and work.

His own particular service was grounded on the reality of wrongdoing; that of Christ was worried with transgression's evacuation. Christ was God's "Sheep." Hostory (Exod. 12:3) and prediction (Isa. 53:7) join in giving the foundation to this title. The day by day sanctuary penances might be as a top priority too.

At the point when John the Baptist focuses to Jesus and shouts, "See, the Lamb of God, who takes away the transgression of the world!" (John 1:29), it is imperative for us to recollect that he talks as a great part of the compelling warrior calf of Malachi 4 who will vanquish abhorrent as of the sheep of Isaiah 53 who was to shoulder upon himself human sin.

We should not miss this unmistakably prophetically calamitous fixing in the message of John the Baptist. John resembles Elijah in challenge with the four hundred bogus prophets of Baal. We feel this ceaseless feeling of fight in John the Baptist and in his forecasts of the part that the person who is both prior and then afterward him will take.

31-34. At the point when Jesus went to John's sanctification, the Baptist did not remember Him (cf. Luke 1:80), however he had gotten an indication of distinguishing proof from God - the Spirit plunging from paradise like a bird and staying on Him. Alongside the sign was given a word concerning the work He ought to perform with the wonderful hardware this given - He would sanctify through water with the Spirit.

Such a one, John knew, could be no not as much as the Son of God. Nobody of lesser stature could make such definitive us of the perfect Spirit. John gave three sterling declarations to Christ's individual and work. As the Lamb, His main goal was to be one of recovery. As baptizer with the Spirit, He would found the Church. As

Son of God, He would be deserving of love and acquiescence.

This is the second way John plans for Christ. It is spoken to in the immersion he offered to the general population who came to hear Him. His absolution is an indication of contrition and planning for the happening to the Lord. It has moral ramifications which turn out to be clear in his peaceful direction to the officers in Luke 3, yet it is in the meantime prophetic.

Take note of that in the Gospel of John, the essayist does not by any stretch of the imagination clarify the contrition subject but instead stresses the prophetic component: "I cam sanctifying through water with water, that he may be uncovered to Israel" (John 1:31).

That is, John's immersion as a custom indicated the Lord, as did his words. John's sanctification is the occasion before the occasion, similarly as his part is to resemble the companion of the husband who cheers to see his companion's wedding occur.

This is the means by which John the Baptist depicts his own particular service in his discourse with the Pharisees (John 3:25). In this sense John's submersion is uplifting news, and his stern words are uplifting news in that they bring us "exhausted and exhausted to the Redeemer" (Pascal, 1941).

This is his main goal - to point broken and debilitated mankind to the Light. "We can't hear the last word until we have heard the beside the last word" (Bonhoeffer, 1972).

John the Baptist is critical in that he plays a baffling, strongly individual part toward Jesus himself. Every Gospel lets us know of the absolution of Jesus by John - that wondrous confusion, where Jesus, who had no compelling reason to submit for a submersion of atonement, yet demands that John purify through water him at Jordan.

It is in this accommodation of Jesus, his aggregate distinguishing proof with the hordes of conventional individuals whohad additionally go to the stream, that a sign is given by God both to Jesus and to John: "This is my cherished son......" John is advantaged to partake in that puzzle. "I have seen and have borne witness" (John 1:34).

35-36. These verses are transitional. They advise us that John had followers and furthermore that he wanted to transfer them to Jesus. This was a vital piece of his work as trailblazer (forerunner), as the rest of the part confirms.

The Gathering Of Disciples
(1:37-51)

John's unselfish longing to celebrate Christ proved to be fruitful among his own adherents. With no summon or proposal from him notwithstanding his declaration, two supporters took after Jesus. One is recognized as Andrew. Quiet in regards to the name of alternate focuses to the author of the Gospel, who withholds his name out of unobtrusiveness.

This anonymous individual is basically portrayed as one of the supporters of John the Baptist. We trust he is the supporter John. This is the most intelligent conclusion in the light of the resolute administer took after all through this Gospel, which does not name the Apostle John in wherever but rather alludes to him by roundabout means.

This component, alluded to as the Johannine signature, gives more support to the custom of the early church which attributes this Gospel to the Apostle John, the most youthful of the followers' band, sibling of James, and a relative of Andrew and Peter (Palmer, 1978).

37-42. They took after Jesus. Accordingly, the physical demonstration express the goal to take after Jesus in an otherworldly sense. What look for ye? Such a question could be a repel, however not when talked generous. The counter question, Where dwellest thou? like their tailing him, could recommend a more profound sense - What is the mystery of your otherworldly life and power?

His home not have lured them, but rather the grand chat that took after waited as a fragrant memory. A long time later John recollected the hour of day - four toward the evening.

41. The significance of "first" is misty. No further movement by Andrew is expressed. Potentially first is proposed to recommend that the other pupil (John) similarly searched out his sibling James, who seems ahead of schedule in the Synoptic accounts as a supporter of Jesus (Mark 1:16-20). "Findeth".... found. The story is bursting at the seams with the delight of revelation (cf. John 1:43-45).

Messias, the Hebrew expression for "blessed

one," has its partner in the Greek word Christ. Did Andrew set out to call Jesus the Christ on the grounds that the Baptist had so distinguished Him to his devotees, or as a result of the hours spent in Jesus' organization? 42. Andrew's own work started early and with his own kinfolk. The change of name from Simon to Cephas, the Aramaic for Peter, which means stone (or shake), likely signifies a guaranteed change from shortcoming to solidness and quality (Luke 22:31, 32).

43. Again the change of day is noted (cf. 1:29, 35 rather than the nonappearance of such components in the Prologue). This time Jesus does the discovering (cf. Luke 19:10), and gives a summon to Philip to take after (difference John 1:37).

45-51. Philip vindicated Jesus' trust in him as a follower by discovering Nathanael and breathing to him his conviction that Jesus of Nazareth was the hotly anticipated One who satisfied the forecasts Moses and the prophets. On may observer to the Lord regardless of the possibility that his comprehension is inadequate or even flawed.

Jesus of Nazareth uncovered himself in a

matter of seconds as the magnificent Son of man (v. 51). Indeed, even Nathanael came rapidly to see that the child of Joseph was the Son of God (v. 49). Nathanael's first drive was to uncertainty that Nazareth was fit for creating any good thing, significantly less the Messiah (v. 46). This does not really infer that the town had an awful notoriety, but instead proposes the immaterial character of the place.

Come and See. Experience is superior to contention. An Israelite without cleverness proposes a complexity to Jacob, who got to be Israel just by a change understanding. A similar infiltration that read the heart of Simon (v. 42) like an open book and punctured to the internal existence of Nathanael (vv. 47, 48) was presently unconditionally recognized in the last's admission Son of God.... Ruler of Israel.

The shade of the fig tree, a calm withdraw for a respectful soul, had been noiselessly shared by the perceiving Christ. Philip understood that the educator must be more than he found in Him. Also, the end was not yet, for the Savior guaranteed more noteworthy things. Jacob was still out of sight (v. 51). His vision of blessed messengers at Bethel would be outperformed as the supporters (ye) came to find in the Son of man the one to whom paradise was open (cf. Matt. 3:16) and the person who, as Mediator, connections paradise and earth.

Son of man. A title signifying an otherworldly, radiant figure in Dan. 7:13 and in the Jewish apocalypses, was Jesus' favored technique for assigning himself, as indicated by the Gospels. This name was desirable over "Savior" since it didn't propose political yearnings along lines of a transient kingdom, for example, most Jews were searching for.

The glory of the Son (John 1:14); found to some degree by these early adherents (vv. 39, 46), was to unfurl all the more from this point forward.

CHAPTER
TWO

Invitation To A Wedding
(2:1-11)

This concise come back to Galilee was not set apart by open service, but rather included an occurrence that bears on the developing of followers' trust in Jesus, proceeding with the accentuation of John 1. Some light is tossed on our Lord's connection to his mom and furthermore on his state of mind toward social life (cf. Matt. 11:19). The transforming of the water into wine is noted as his first marvel.

1. The "third day" appears to identify with 1:43. Two days or more would have been required for the voyage to Cana, which was situated around seven and a half miles north of Nazareth. John takes note of the nearness of the mother of Jesus at the marriage. His evasion of the name Mary here and in 19:26 might be because of a limitation like what shrouds his own particular name. He had an extraordinary connection to Mary (19:27).

2. It is questionable whether Jesus planned the voyage keeping in mind the end goal to be available for the marriage or whether the welcome to him and his pupils came after their

entry in Galilee. In the event that the last is the right option, the exhaustion of the supply of wine might be promptly clarified. Different visitors may have arrived out of the blue too. Nathanael, whose house was in Cana, perhaps had something to do with the courses of action.

Late reviews into first century wedding traditions may help us to comprehend this question to Jesus by his mom. Wedding dining experiences would normally most recent seven days, and the visitors were required to bring a present of wine. It is conceivable that Jesus and his devotees (disciples) had neglected to carry with them their present, and his mom expects just to help Jesus to remember that oversight (Brown, 1970).

3-5. Mary came to Jesus with the greetings that the wine supply had been depleted. In his answer, the utilization of "woman" does not include slight (cf. 19:26). What have I to do with thee? The words demonstrate division of intrigue and seen to recommend a measure of censure. Mary may have anticipated that Jesus would utilize the circumstance to point out himself in a way that would have advance his Messianic program.

Yet, his hour had not yet come. Later references indicate the cross as the point of convergence of great importance (7:30; 8:20; 12:23; 13:1; 17:1). Jesus needed his mom to comprehend that the previous relationship among them (Luke 2:51) was at an end. She was not to meddle in his central goal.

Mary carefully did not debate the matter. On the off chance that she couldn't order him, she could teach the hirelings to comply with his headings. Subsequently she demonstrated her trust in him.

Whatever the purpose behind Mary's underlying explanation to Jesus, the Lord's answer is bigger than her question, and goes a long ways past what the peruser may anticipate from the discourse. He starts with a typical Semitism, actually, "What to me to you." The "O Woman" is not impolite but rather a title in conventional utilization. At that point he grows his sentence a long ways past the normal furthest reaches of the discussion by the overwhelming sentence, "My hour has not yet come."

How are we to translate this discourse? One aftereffect of this experience is that the relationship amongst Jesus and his mom has been changed. There is an unexpected separating of Jesus from his regular connections in a path like the Nazareth occurrence recorded in Luke's Gospel, aside from that the town-mates of Jesus in Luke's record (Luke 4:16-30) don't trust Jesus' choice, while his mom does.

Inside John's Gospel the mother of the Lord won't again play a noteworthy part until the hour at the cross when Jesus Christ gently recognizes her to the pupil John and John to her (John 19).

Mary reacts to the announcement of Jesus as though she comprehends and is fulfilled. She pulls back from the occasion, subsequent to educating the hirelings to do what Jesus lets them know.

6-8. In meeting the crisis, Jesus made utilization of "six waterpots of stone, for example, Jews utilized for refining the washing of the hands previously, then after the fact suppers, and different stately washings. Each would have held around twenty gallons.

At the point when these had been filled, Jesus taught the hirelings to "draw out." This appears to allude to the demonstration of removing water from the extensive holders by plunging from them and putting into littler containers.

What was attracted was then conveyed to the legislative leader of the devour. Some consider that the goveernor was minimal more than a head servant; others find in him a companion of the groom who was asked for to go about as an emcee (cf. Eccelesiasticus 32:1 ff.).

9,10. An essence of the wine guaranteed this functionary that it was prevalent quality, so much better that he felt obliged than compliment the spouse for treating his visitors with irregular thought, giving them great wine toward the finish of the devour, when many would be so filled as not to have the capacity to recognize whether the wine was great or inside.

The deficiency of wine was soothed by Jesus' mediation. The more profound truth is that, typically, Judaism is here uncovered as insufficient (in its worry upon stately washings to the disregard of otherworldly matters, and in its exhaustion, demonstrated by the void water containers), though Christ brings totality of gift of the most elevated sort (cf. 7:37-39). Besides, he does it without pointing out himself, an invigorating case.

11. "Start of Miracles." This announcement disproves the fanciful Gospels which report

childhood marvels by Jesus. The word for supernatural occurrence, which John utilizes all through, means sign, demonstrating that outward demonstration is proposed to uncover the reason behind it, tossing light on the individual of Christ or his work.

"Radiance" for this situation is a term pointing out the strength of Jesus to achieve a profound change, as recommended by the changing of water into wine (cf. 11:40). His pupils accepted on him. Rather than the leader of the disciples; who was described by obliviousness (v. 9) and to the workers, who knew about the supernatural occurrence (v. 9), the followers were moved to confidence. Only they really benefitted by the sign.

The First Visit To Jerusalem And Judea (2:12-3:36)

The Cleaning Of The Temple (2:12-22)

Despite the fact that this is not called a sign, it was a more groundbreaking occasion than the supernatural occurrence at Cana, for it bore straightforwardly on the mission of Jesus, being a Messianic demonstration of an open sort. At the end of the day Judaism was appeared to be insufficient, and even degenerate, for the Father's home was being debased.

Jesus related the episode to his revival (vv. 19-21). It uncovered the unbelief of the Jews (vv. 18-20) and the confidence of the pupils (disciples) (v. 22). As an occasion, it ought to be recognized from a later purging before Jesus' passing (Mark 11:15-19).

12. This verse is transitional. The significance of Capernaum for Jesus' service is worried in the Synoptic Gospels. He made it his Galilean central station "his own city" (Matt. 9:1). The crack with his Brethren (siblings) had not yet created (John 7:3-5).

13. The Jew's passover (cf. 2:6). At the end of the day John is determined to uncovering the insufficiencies of Judaism. The sacrosanct commemoration of the deliverance from Egypt was being mishandled. Since it was Jesus' propensity to watch the national celebrations, as it had been the propensity for Joseph and Mary (Luke 2:41), he went up to Jerusalem.

14-16. Jesus the admirer now turned into a reformer. The Sanhedrin was allowing, and most likely controlling for its own monetary premium, an activity in conciliatory creatures and cash evolving. This activity carried on in the expansive territory known as the Court of the Gentiles, was to the benefit of the pioneer, since he could get his relinquish here as opposed to carry it with him.

Probably there was an assurance that the creature was "without flaw." Various sorts of coinage could be changed at the tables for the Palestinian half shekel required for the yearly sanctuary assess. This movement transformed the Temple into a bazaar of exchange. Frustrated at the blasphemy, Jesus went without hesitation.

Rapidly he molded a scourge out of the ropes lying about the place. With this whip he drove the men (them) and the creatures out of the sanctuary zone and surprise the tables of cash changers, sending their coins ringing here and there on the asphalt.

The pigeons couldn't well be driven. It was vital just that their proprietors take them out. Such strenuous measures required avocation, and it was found in this, that the Father's home had been debased into a place of stock. The Lord had come all of a sudden to his Temple and had decontaminated the children of Levi (Mal. 3:1-3).

A more profound lesson than the evacuation of defilement may have been expected by this removal of conciliatory creatures, even the suspicion of the day when the Temple and its penances would be gone and the last give up of The Lamb of God be accomplished (cf. 2:21; 1:29).

17. The episode reviewed to the supporters an entry in a Messianic song (69:9) - "For the energy of thine house hath gobbled me up; and rebukes of them that censured thee are fallen." An indication might be found here that this enthusiasm, which cost him restriction right now, would in the end cost him his life (cf. John 2:19).

18-22. Such extraordinary activity rapidly brought a request from the Jews (pioneers) that Jesus deliver an incontestable sign to demonstrate that he had expert for his direct. He generally opposed such a request (6:30; Matt.16:1). This time he was substance to indicate what's to come. Demolish this sanctuary. The metaphorical character of the expression is apparent, from John 2:21, as well as from the articulate impossibility that the Jews would wreck their own particular Temple.

These words are not to be taken as an order or welcome, however are in the way of a hypotesis- "On the off chance that you crush, I will raise up." In three days is comparable to "on the third day." Taking him truly, the Jews felt that his announcement was silly, since the Temple had required forty-six years to construct.

Herod had started its recreation in 20 B.C. Some work still stayed to be done, however the structure was adequately entire to be talked about as manufactured. (For the utilization of the figure sanctuary for the body, see I Corinthians 6:19.). This prediction advanced confidence with respect to the followers, yet not until after the restoration of their Lord from the dead (cf. John 12:16).

The Signs
(2:23-35)

This segment is transitional, having extraordinarily close association with the accompanying episode. It is synopsis in nature, envisioning Jesus as performing different signs in Jerusalem that are left undescribed. The vital thing is the reaction, which for this situation was not rank unbelief, nor the full trust in Christ credited to the devotees, yet something that might be called supernatural occurrence confidence.

Its inadmissible character is ensured by the way that Jesus did not submit himself unto these individuals, since he knew the human heart and observed the absence of real trust. For fairly comparable occasions, see 8:30-59; 12:42, 43.

CHAPTER

THREE

The Encounter With Nicodemus
(3:1-15)

As opposed to the numerous in Jerusalem who "accepted" yet to whom Jesus declined to confer himself, Nicodemus lingers as one to whom the Lord opened his heart, one who turned into a genuine pupil. In the meantime the entry stresses a prior subject - the restrictions of current Judaism - by demonstrating the powerlessness of this pioneer to grasp the otherworldly truth articulated by Jesus.

1-2. The "Pharisees" were the religious pioneers of the country. Nicodemus had a place with this gathering, as well as was a leader of the Jews, an individual from the Sanhedrin. He came to see Jesus by night, likely out of practicality. The official state of mind toward the Nazarene, after the purifying of the Temple, more likely than not been one of solid restriction.

John might propose likewise the visual deficiency of this man concerning divine things. Nicodemus was prepared to surrender that Jesus was an educator sent of God, the marvels being witness. This could imply that he was a prophet of more prominent power than John, who did no marvel.

"We know" recommends that others were thinking along comparable lines. Regardless of whether there is any proposed indicate that Jesus may be the Messiah is not clear.

3-4. In the brain of Nicodemus the wonders may well have been signs of the fast happening to the kingdom of God in a political sense. Be that as it may, Jesus presented a completely extraordinary idea of the kingdom, with the signs indicating a profound rule of God. To be "conceived once more" is to be conceived once more, from above.

Nicodemus was nonplused. He realized that a man can not be conceived over again in a physical sense. Maybe Jesus implied that it is similarly as unimaginable for one who is old to change his viewpoint and his ways.

5-8. Jesus now depicted the new birth as far as "water" and "Soul." Of these two, Spirit is the more urgent (see v. 6). Water may well allude to the accentuation of John the Baptist on contrition and purifying from transgression as the essential foundation for, even the negative side of the new birth.

Less regular is any inference to the Word (I Peter 1:23). The positive fixing is the infusion of new creation life by the recovering force of the Spirit (cf. Titus 3:5). Ye must be conceived once more. This is not simply an individual but rather a general request. The need lies in the insufficiency of the substance.

This incorporates what is only common and what is corrupt man as he is naturally introduced to this world and carries on with his life separated from God's effortlessness. Substance can just replicate itself as tissue, and this can't pass gather with God (cf. Romans 8:8). The law of proliferation is "after its kind." So similarly the Spirit produces soul, an existence conceived, supported, and developed by the Spirit of God.

On the off chance that this spells riddle, let it be perceived that there is puzzle in nature too. "Wind" (pneuma, an indistinguishable word from for "Soul") produces discernible impacts as it blows, yet its source and future developments stay covered up. So the reclaimed life shows itself as something compelling, however opposing examination by the normal man (cf. I Corinthians 2:15).

9-10. The perplexity of Nicodemus drew a tender reprimand from Jesus. Would it be able to be that an ace (lit. the educator) of Israel did not know these things? They were not new (Ezekiel 11:19). An otherworldly kingdom and a profound life to match it are not remote to the instructing of the Old Testament.

11-13. Besides, others could vouch for the truth of these things-we talk. Jesus was satisfied to connect his devotees with himself. Ye (you and others like you) get not the witness. "Natural things" are the things as of now talked about, of otherworldly birth and life. "Glorious things" are matters which the Son of man, by his descending from paradise, needed to uncover as new and particular (cf. Matt. 11:25-27). The last four expressions of 3:13 are not contained in the main original copies.

14-15. There is another must offering an explanation to the basic of the new birth (cf. 3:7). the lifting up of the Son of man can't well allude to Ascension, in perspective of the height of the audacious serpent on a post (Numbers 21:8), with which it is here thought about. The mention is to the cross (John 12:32, 33).

As men harassed with the nibble of the

destructive serpent looked with anticipation and trust toward that which took after the reptile that had set the infection of death streaming in their veins, so delinquents must look in confidence to Christ their substitute, who came in the similarity of evil fragile living creature and for transgression (Romans 8:3).

The issue of such confidence is "everlasting life." Apart from this confidence one must "die." This is not demolition but rather the deplorability of being cut off endlessly from God. Clearly Nicodemus acknowledged the notice and the test (John 7:50, 51; 19:39, 40). Now, it appears, the expressions of Jesus stop and those of John resume' according to the style, which has a few analogies to different parts of the Gospel where John is irrefutably in charge of the material.

Issues Hidden In The Gospel Message (3:16-21)

Cherish for transgression prompts men to dismiss the light of Christ, though the individuals who welcome the light are prepared to put their trust in him.

16-17. John develops the announcement

of Jesus (3:15), controlling whosoever, die, believeth, unceasing (everlasting additionally deciphers a similar Greek word) life. The additional components are the affection for God and the subsequent giving of his Son, who is portrayed as the main sired. This implies special, exceptional. Children by selection don't get to be individuals from the Godhead.

The expansiveness of the awesome love is accentuated in that its protest is the (entire) world. In spite of the fact that the happening to Christ included judgment, as whatever is left of this segment bears witness to, the immediate reason for that coming, laying on the heavenly love, was not judgment but rather salvation (3:17).

18-21. The devotee to Christ does not come into judgment for his wrongdoings either now or later on (the verb frame is sufficiently fexible to cover both angles). Then again, the person who declines to trust stands judged by prudence of that refusal. He has chosen his own particular destiny.

The fundamental thought in judgment is a qualification, a detachment; and the happening to Christ as the light demonstrated an awesome separating impact. Rather than reacting to the adoration for God by cherishing His Son, most men adored the obscurity in inclination to the light since they were connected to their example of life, which was detestable (fiendish).

In 3:20 "underhandedness" is an alternate word, meaning what is ethically useless. The guilty party knows he is enmeshed in wrong, yet declines to progress into the light of Christ keeping in mind that his deeds, which he cherishes, be uncovered. Then again, the person who goes to the light is depicted as one who doeth truth. He acts as per what he knows to be correct (cf. 18:37).

This adjustment to what he knows to be reality sets him up to progress into the full light of Christ and be spared. Every one of his works are fashioned in God, who has been driving him to this peak of confidence (cf. 1:47).

Further Witness From John the Baptist (3:22-30)

The way that Jesus and his devotees carried on a work of lecturing and purifying through water in Judea while John and his adherents led a comparable work in another range prompted to the doubt that the two were in rivalry. John denied this earnestly, readily playing a part of subordination to Jesus.

22-24. After these things. The Nicodemus scene is finished. The place where there is Judea is named in qualification from Jerusalem, where Jesus had been working (2:13-3:21). Jesus' submersing action presupposes lecturing. His connection to sanctification appears to have been just supervisory (cf. 4:2; I Corinthians 1:14).

Aenon and Salim have not thought to have been a couple of miles east of Mouont Gerizim, as opposed to south of Bethshan in the upper Jordan Valley. They came. Individuals for the most part, who were keen on John's message. John's detainment is noted here as something natural to the perusers, since it is accounted for in all the Synoptic Gospels.

25-26. John's pupils were drawn into a squabble with a few Jews (there is great reason for perusing a Jew here) over the issue of cleaning. The essayist does not let us know whether this implies refinement when all is said in done as rehearsed by the Jews, or the absolution honed by John and Jesus over against those purifyings, or the sanctifications of John and Jesus as opposed to each other.

Maybe the latter is the in all probability, in perspective of the spin-off. They came. Most likely John's devotees. He. Inability to specify Jesus all the more unquestionably appears like examined deterioration. John's followers were worried over the disappearing position of their pioneer. The group were presently thronging Jesus.

27-30. The Baptist despised any considered competition amongst himself and Jesus. His own place, given by God (from paradise), was not that of the Christ but rather that of the herald (v. 28). His position was not that of the Bridegroom, who ought to take the general population of God to himself. This was saved for Another. Or maybe, he was the companion of the Bridegroom. It was the capacity of such a man to go about as go-between in making the marriage courses of action.

His euphoria was vicarious-investment in the satisfaction of the prepare as another family was framed. John's work was done in propelling the work of Jesus. He could sanctify through water just with water, not with the Spirit. He could declare the happening to the kingdom yet not go into it himself.

His cause needed to blur, in the way of the case, as that of Jesus expanded (v. 30). This was God's arrangement. Thus Jesus, notwithstanding being better than Judaism, was better than the development that focused about John (cf. Acts 19:1-3).

The Credentials Of Christ
(3:31-36)

Here the Evangelist thinks about the distinctives of Jesus, particularly as these set him apart from the Baptist. He has a radiant inception, which puts him above earthlings and natural things (cf. 3:13). He bears his declaration to what he sees and listens, a declaration to radiant things (cf. 16:13). Just recover men, those conceived of the Spirit, can value his declaration (Nicodemus was out of sight of John's idea here).

The individuals who do get his declaration require no other verification (cf. I John 5:10). Christ pronounces the expressions of God (John 3:34) as a dedicated witness. The totality of those words, and additionally their exactness, is ensured by the unmeasured endowment of the Spirit conceded to him.

The first proposes that through him a similar Spirit is given to others without measure (cf. 1:33). Encourage, the Christ is the extraordinary protest of God's affection and is the caretaker of heavenly wealth (cf. 16:15; Matt. 11:27). He is the touchstone of interminable life or tolerating fierceness (John 3:36).

CHAPTER

FOUR

The Samaritans
(4:1-42)

Samaria, a domain to be dodged if conceivable by Jews, turned into the scene of an otherworldly triumph: a well, a lady, a witness, the triumphant of a gather of Samaritans to confidence. Samaritanism and additionally Judaism required the remedial of Christ; it should have been supplanted by new creation life.

1-4. The developing ubiquity of Jesus, surpassing that of John, started to go to the ears of the Pharisees. To maintain a strategic distance from issue with them right now, Jesus resolved to leave the region and go to into Galilee. This is the place a large portion of his work was done, as per the Synoptic records.

He should experience Samaria. Commonly in John this word focuses to an awesome need, and it might do as such here, showing the need of managing the Samaritans and opening to them the passage to life. Alongside this might be the more apparent need of achieving Galilee by the most direct course.

5-6. Sychar (more probable Sychem, i.e., Shechem) was a couple of miles southeast of the city of Samaria and genuinely near Mount Gerizim and in addition to the ground given by Jacob to Joseph (Gen. 48:22). Jacob left likewise a well as a legacy (John 4:6). This is accounted for to be around eighty-five feet inside and out. Here Jesus, wearied with the adventure and the early afternoon (6th hour) warm, delayed to rest.

7-10. A lady of Samaria. Not a reference to the city of Samaria, which was too far away, yet to the domain of the Samaritans. She came prepared to draw water. Since the town of Sychar had water, it is conceivable that the lady's singular excursion to Jacob's well from everyday shows a types of alienation by the other ladies of the group (cf. 4:18).

Jesus ended the hush with a demand for a drink. It was a characteristic demand in perspective of his exhaustion. It is a piercing indication of our Lord's mankind. Regardless of whether the demand was satisfied or not (the last appears to be more plausible), it prompted to discussion. The flight of the devotees was fortunate, for the lady would not have gone into dialog with Jesus in their nearness.

Two things stunned the lady: that Jesus would make such a demand of a lady, for a rabbi stayed away from contact with ladies out in the open; and especially that he would talk in this way to one who was a Samaritan.

In clarification of her awe, the essayist includes the perception that Jews had no dealings with Samaritans. this can't be taken in an outright sense, for it is discredited by verse 8. It might indicate the terrible feeling between the two individuals. The Jews detested the Samaritans since they were a blended people in blood and in religion, who all things considered had the Pentateuch and maintained to venerate the God of Israel.

A smaller importance has been proposed for the lady's colloquialism - "Jews don't make regular use (of vessels) with Samaritans." This fits the circumstance well (Daube, 1994). In his answer Jesus moved far from his own particular need to recommend that the lady had one which was more profound, one he could supply through the "endowment of God." Some clarify this in individual terms as alluding to Christ himself (3:16), however it is presumably better to make it proportional to "living water." John 7:37-39 is the best critique (cf. Rev. 21:6).

11-12. Thinking as far as the well underneath

them, the lady was astounded. Jesus had no utensil for drawing and the well was profound. At the base was the living (running) water nourished by a spring. Could this rabbi would like to evoke what Jacob secured just by hard drudge? He would in fact be more noteworthy if be could do this.

13-15. Water from the well must be devoured over and over, however the water Christ apportions will so fulfill that one might never thirst. Such is the refreshment of everlasting life. A parallel might be drawn with the rehashed penances of the old agreement and the one-for-all yield of the Lamb of God. As yet misjudging, yet now open, the lady requested such water, that her parcel may be simpler (4:15).

16-18. Prior to the lady could get the endowment of living water, she must be made to acknowledge how frantically she required it. This blessing was for the internal life, which for her situation was void to be sure. Thy husband... no husband.... five husbands.... not thy spouse. The bleak history of her conjugal life was unfurled by Jesus' infiltration and by her own affirmation.

It is likely that separation went into at any

rate a portion of the five connections which went before the last ill-conceived status. Ethically, the lady had been going downhill for quite a while.

19-20. To the lady, Jesus was initial a Jew, then one qualified for be called Sir, and now a prophet. He had investigated her spirit. The reference to revere on adjacent Mount Gerizim, built up in rivalry to that of the Jews at Jerusalem, may have been a diversionary strategy, yet more probable it meant that a heart appetite to know the best approach to God.

21-24. "The hour cometh." In the new request that Christ has come to initiate, the place of love is subordinated to the Person. the essential thing is that men revere the Father, whom the Son has come to pronounce. By utilizing ye, Jesus might envision the change of the Samaritan men. The Samaritan love was a confounded thing (cf. II Kings 17:33).

Salvation is of the Jews as in unique disclosure came to them concerning the correct way to deal with God; and Jesus himself, as the Savior, originated from this individuals (Rom. 9:5). The hour..... presently is. Indeed, even before the new allotment is introduced in its universalistic character, genuine admirers are special to love God as Father in soul and in truth.

Soul appears to look back at Jerusalem and its love regarding letter (the Law), though truth is rather than the insufficient and bogus love of the Samaritans. The new sort of love is basic since God is Spirit (not a Spirit).

25-26. The lady's implication to the Messiah was most likely in light of Deut. 18: 15-18, which was acknowledged by the Samaritans as Scripture. As the prophet second to none, the Messiah would have the capacity to tell.... all things. This thoughtful projection into what's to come was pointless. I that talk unto thee am he.

It would have been risky for Jesus to declare himself in this design among the Jews, where thoughts of Messiahship were politically shaded. Here, clearly, he passed judgment on it to be protected. The seed was planted, and in the nick of time, for the discussion was finished by the arrival of the disciples.

27-30. The disciples wondered that Jesus would break tradition by chatting with the lady (see v. 9). In any case, adoration for their educator kept them from open addressing. Unrestricted by her waterpot, the lady resigned with all speed to the town, her demonstration promising her motivation to return and broadcasting her assurance to have the living water from this time forward.

She accomplished more than Jesus asked, going not to one man, but rather to the men of the place with the news of her energizing knowledge. She didn't attempt to show them, however put an idea in their psyches, stated likely: Is this, perchance, the Christ? The men were adequately inspired to oblige her to the well.

31-38. In the interim the devotees squeezed Jesus to take sustenance, yet he declined on the ground that he had food of which they were unmindful. This, he clarified, was the doing of God's will (v. 34). He had been doing this in their nonattendance, and he had done it in the light of the cross, where he would complete God's delegated work (cf. 17:4; 19:30).

His service was one of both sowing and harvesting. Four months till collect would be the regular domain, however by lifting up their eyes the supporters could see a reap officially white (the moving toward Samaritans), the consequence of his sowing (4:35).

In otherworldly work, sower and collector are usually unique people, who celebrate together in what their consolidated endeavors have fulfilled (vv. 36, 37). Here in Samaria and in numerous different circumstances the followers, despite the fact that not the sowers of the seed, may harvest. Others may incorporate Jesus and the lady of Samaria.

It might be said even Moses may have a place here, as being humanly in charge of embedding the seed of Messianic desire in the heart of the lady.

39-42. Here we learn of the natural product which Christ and the lady could accumulate as sower and collector. Many accepted on the Lord due to the lady's declaration. This prompted to a welcome to remain in their middle, which Christ agreed to accomplish for two days.

Amid those days, other people who had heard the lady's declaration and had been slanted to trust in Jesus turned out to be undeniable devotees due to what they got through his own particular word, i.e., from Jesus' own lips (v. 42). Friend in need of the world - a thankful admission, since it implied that Samaritans and in addition Jews could be spared.

Healing The Nobleman's Son
(4:43-54)

This episode is the main thing of service detailed by John regarding this visit of Jesus to Galilee. The kid, lying wiped out at Capernaum, was mended by Jesus' assertion when He was at Cana, miles away.

43-45. The importance of Jesus' own nation has been greatly talked about. Conceivably the most straightforward arrangement is that Galilee in general is implied. An absence of respect was to be relied upon there rather than the developing prevalence agreed him in Judea (3:26; 4:1).

The way that Galileans who had been at Jerusalem and had seen his supernatural occurrences there were prepared to welcome him doesn't place them in the class of genuine and changeless adherents (cf. 2:23-25; 4:48). Inevitably the Galileans would abandon him (6:66).

While at Cana, Jesus had a visit from a specific aristocrat (basilikos, showing an illustrious figure or one in imperial administration). The father's expectation of getting mending from Jesus for his child appears to have been founded on contact with Galileans who had seen our Lord's wonders at Jerusalem (4:47; cf. v. 45).

Having ventured from Capernaum to Cana, the father made rehashed and dire demand that Jesus would descend and recuperate the kid. Jesus communicated expect that the father, similar to such a large number of others was so distracted with the report of miracles played out that he would not accept.

More critical than the kid's wellbeing was the father's confidence. The father's answer inhales the distress of need (cf. Check 9:22-24). Jesus substantiated himself deserving of confidence and furthermore thoughtful to the suppliant's sentiments - Go thy way; thy child liveth. His confidence growing quick, the man trusted the expression of Christ separated from any unmistakable sign, and went his direction fulfilled.

51-54. The workers of the aristocrat, tensely watching their lord's child in his nonappearance, noticed the radical change in his condition and began to meet the father with the uplifting news. The aristocrat himself, officially soothing in his confidence, was intrigued now in taking in the season of the change.

When he thought about the season of the flight of the fever with the season of his meeting with Jesus, he knew the recuperating was no mischance. He himself accepted. Confidence spread to the whole family unit (v. 53). At the principal Cana supernatural occurrence the followers had accepted. The second wonder from a similar spot brought about a more extensive hover of confidence.

CHAPTER

FIVE

The Healing Of The Lame
Man In Jerusalem
(5:1-16)

Both the time and the place of this marvel
have been tremendously debated. In the event
that this feast of the Jews was the Passover, then
four such feasts are specified in John, making
the service three and a half to four years, if
John records them all (the others are 2:23; 6:4;
11:55). Since the best composition experts do
not have the clear article, some feasts other than
the Passover is likely expected.

The place of the supernatural occurrence
may now be related to some certainty, taking
after the removal in 1888 of such a pool as John
portrays, situated in the northeastern piece of
Jerusalem, close to the Church of St. Anne.
The different readings in the original copy for
the name of the pool are confusing. Beth-zatha
is very much bore witness to. It presumably
signifies "Place of Olives."

Another Account recounts the second visit
of Jesus to Jerusalem. The time is not given
to us for this situation, with the exception of
by the inconclusive remark that there was "a

devour." Perhaps this is the Feast of Weeks-we can't be sure.

John recounts a pool in Jerusalem, close to the sheep entryway, called "Bethesda" in Hebrew. John's particular land documentation has been as of late approved from two sources. The copper scroll found at Qumram has named the pool on the eastern slope in Jerusalem as "Wager 'Esda," place of the streaming" (Milik, 1959, 1962). Added to this, archeologists have effectively exhumed the pool site and have discovered its five porticoes (five yards) as John portray them.

2-4. The five yards or porticoes, now revealed, shielded an awesome organization of debilitated, some visually impaired, others faltering, other wilted, i.e., deadened. They were there in any desire for being recuperated when the water was vexed. While our composition convention is with the end goal that the finish of verse 3 and all of verse 4 can't be viewed as a feature of the first content of John, this segment is an early custom.

J. Rendel Harris fouond confirm in a few places all through the East of a superstition such that at the New Year a blessed messenger was required to mix the water in specific territories, empowering one individual to acquire mending by being the first to get into the water after the unsettling influence.

On this premise he judged the devour of this section to have been Trumpets, reporting the New Year (Westcott, 1896). The remaining parts of the Church of St. Anne incorporate the figure of a holy messenger, vouching for this conviction and the custom of looking for recuperating under these uncommon conditions.

5-7. There is nothing to show the exact way of the infirmity that had held this wiped out man for such a large number of years, aside from that he couldn't move without offer assistance. It is not in any way likely that he stayed there this time. Or maybe, he was brought there when the moving of the water was normal.

Jesus knew. Since nothing is said of the impartation of learning by others, we are to infer that here, as with Nathanael and the lady of Samaria, Jesus perceived the genuine situation by his own energy of recognition. Shrink thou be made entirety? For this situation Jesus stepped up.

The question was not unnecessary, for some who are interminable invalids have no trust of cure. Others utilize their ailment as a method for inspiring sensitivity, consequently would prefer truly not to be mended. The wiped out man had the yearning for mending, yet did not have the methods (v. 7). 8,9. Three charges by Jesus infer the impartation of quality. The mending was prompt. Bed. Sleeping pad or bed.

10-13. Rapidly the mending turned into the subject of debate, since it had been performed on the sabbath day. The Jews. For this situation not the average citizens, but rather their rulers (cf. 1:19). Clearly they watched the man strolling through the lanes toward his home, conveying his bed.

This disregarded the Sabbath rest (Jer. 17:21). In his disarray, the mended man could just clarify that his promoter had told him to do this very thing (John 5:11). He couldn't recognize the healer, for he had not scholarly his name, and now it appeared to be difficult to discover, for Jesus had left the scene.

14-16. Since he was not blameworthy of purposeful infringement of the Law, the recuperated man was allowed to go his direction. Later on he continued to the Temple to offer gratitude for his mending. There Jesus discovered him and gave him a message of caution. Sin no more, keeping in mind that a more awful thing come unto thee.

Physical recuperating at Jesus' hands might should incorporate pardoning of sins (cf. Stamp 2:9-12). This pardoning must not be daintily acknowledged. The more awful thing is left vague, and the notice is the more compelling consequently.

Coming back to the Jews, the man distinguished Jesus as the healer, likely not on the grounds that he had resented Jesus' notice, but since he felt a commitment, as an individual from the group, to supply data looked for by the specialists.

This drove the rulers to mistreat Jesus. To them his blame as a culprit was plain. He had damaged the Sabbath. These things are not characterized. The verb is "he was doing," just as to recommend there were other comparable grievances. The words and tried to kill him lack sufficient manuscript authority.

Jesus' Self-Defense
(5:17-47)

The sanctuary pioneers are threatening for two reasons: initially, in light of the fact that

Jesus broke the Sabbath and second, since he "likewise called God his Father, making himself level with God." John records for us a long showing talk in which Jesus considers important the philosophical protests made against his recuperating follow up on the Sabbath.

The fourth edict of Moses' Law tells Israel, "Six days you might work, and do all your work; yet the seventh day is a Sabbath to the Lord your God; in it you should not do any work" (Deut. 5:13-14). "Sabbath" is a transliteration of a Hebrew word signifying "stop," so the charge is clear; it is given by God to support us since it is his will that there might be a mood of life amongst work and rest.

This summon had gone up against exceptionally specific significance when of the primary century and would stay all through the principal century a consistent wellspring of debate among the pioneers of Jewish however.

We have records of a meeting toward the finish of the time of four recognized rabbis, Gamaliel II, Joshua ben Channaniah, Eliezer ben Azariah, and Aquiba. They met in Rome to examine the question - that being said still a fervently one-regardless of whether God watches his own law, with unique concentration upon Sabbath Law.

These rabbis concurred with customary Jewish thought communicated by Philo of Alexandria, a first century Jewish author and a contemporary of New Testament essayists, that God himself does not lay on the Sabbath.

Philo expresses: "For God never stops making, yet as it is the property of God to make." He additionally clarifies that the celestial "rest" of God does not imply that God swears off doing great deeds or from his part as judge of all (Dodd, 1953)(see Dodd's work for a broad examination of first century Jewish thought on this matter).

The accompanying talk manages the expert of Jesus, which he grounds in his uncommon connection to the Father.

17-18. Since working was the reason for conflict, Jesus focuses to God as a proceeding with laborer. Despite the fact that the Father rested from his inventive movement (Gen. 2:2), he should work to manage the universe. He should work additionally to acquire the new creation. The significance is by all accounts that at the same time the Father had been working, the Son had been working as well.

This was a more prominent claim than to state that the Father had been working and now the Son was accepting the weight. The Jews got the suggestion: Jesus was stating that God was his own particular Father, along these lines asserting balance with God. This was more regrettable than taking a shot at the Sabbath. Such disrespect called for death (cf. John 7:30).

19-20. This talk proceeded without obvious intrusion from the Jews. No haughtiness denoted Jesus' claim, which was adjusted by entire reliance on and subordination to the Father. This is genuine sonship, Jesus calls attention to, to gain from the Father and duplicate what is seen (v. 19).

The Son's observation is helped by the Father's disclosure to him concerning the importance for goodness' sake that are finished by the Father. To show the truth of the relationship between the two, more prominent works than these (the mending of the inept man and comparable signs) will be imminent.

21-24. One of these more noteworthy works is the raising of the dead (v. 21). Obviously this is as much an imaginative go about as the first impartation of life. In the event that the Son has energy to revive whom he will, he shares of the Father's energy. Judgment is a moment circle in which the perfect specialist is show.

This capacity has been offered over to the Son. Take note of that restoration and judgment are firmly related eschatological capacities, of which there were foregleams amid Christ's service, for example, the revival of Lazarus and the judgment upon Satan (16:11).

Behind the sharing of expert is the outline that the Son might get respect similarly with the Father. To reject it is to disrespect the Father (5:23). The two subjects of (1) life out of death and (2) judgment are currently united (v. 24); however the revival here is profound, not physical, specifically, cooperation in everlasting life.

One must accept on the One who sent the Son, not in the feeling of by-passing the Son, yet as seeing that confidence in the Father and in the Son are indissoluble.

25-30. Jesus develops his energy to give profound stimulating (vv. 25, 26). This work has a place with the future, he says, but at the same time is presently going on (note diverge from v. 28). The dead for this situation are not in the graves, as in verse 28, but rather are dead in wrongdoing. Their enlivening comes through hearing the voice of the Son of God (cf. v. 24 - he that heareth my assertion; 6:60; 18:37). In nothing is the Son autonomous of the Father, even in the crucial matter of life itself (5:26).

At the end of the day Christ puts forward his power in judgment (v. 27). Child of man is utilized here, as it is in Daniel 7:13; regarding judgment and domain. It is a specialized eschatological term, meaning more than humankind yet including it. As Lord of revival, Jesus will summon all from their graves (cf. Acts 24:15).

In perspective of Revelation 20:4-5, we are to think about a period interim between these two periods of restoration. The doing great incorporates having confidence in the Son of God, even as doing shrewdness incorporates the dismissal of the Son and his cases. Punishment. Actually judgment.

The following verse (John 5:30) is transitional, holding the say of judgment from the current setting and reckoning by its utilization of the primary individual of the pronoun the material that takes after. The Son alone has this interesting connection to the Father.

31-40. In this section the topic of witness is highest. If Jesus somehow happened to hold up under observer to himself, he says, in segregation from the Father's witness, it would be untrue on the grounds that deficient and unsupported. He couldn't anticipate that the Jews will get it.

In any case, his witness is really not of this sort (cf. 8:18). Another takes the stand, the Father. Lamentably the Jews don't perceive the Father's witness (cf. 7:28; 8:19), as are weakened for perceiving the bolster it conveys to Jesus' cases (5:32).

A moment witness was John the Baptist, who was searched out by the Jews themselves for his declaration (1:26; 3:26). This witness was as per reality, as the plummet of the Spirit upon Jesus demonstrated. However accommodating such witness may have been in driving others to a correct assessment of himself, Jesus did not depend upon it as important to his own consciousness of persona and mission (5:34).

However John's statement, recognized by Jesus, was proposed to help these individuals to be spared. Jesus here portrays John as the copying and sparkling light. As smoldering, he bit by bit blurred (3:30), yet as sparkling, he empowered men to see their need of the more prominent Light (cf. 1:8).

All things considered, his declaration outlasted him. For a season. John's prevalence did not keep going long. A third observer to Jesus is found in his works, which were given to him by the Father to perform, keeping in mind the end goal to confirm his perfect mission (v. 36). Wrap up. Nothing speculative or deficient. The works arranged the path for the work, which we now know was done on Calvary and which needs no correction.

As a part of the more prominent witness, our Lord incorporates the declaration of the Father contained in the Scriptures (5:37-40). This he plainly recognizes from the Father's quick declaration to him (v. 32). The detachment of God, because of his deep sense of being (v. 37) is overcome to an extensive degree through the disclosure of himself in the Scriptures of the Old Testament.

However, that word had not flourished in Jesus' listeners. The verification lies in the way that they had not gotten him of whom the Word talks (5:38). Inquiry might be either demonstrative or basic in this occasion, yet the feeling of the entry supports the characteristic.

The Jews were in the propensity for looking the Scriptures since they perceived that these contain the mystery of endless life. Colleague with the Law was the objective of Jewish devotion; so the composed Word had a tendency to wind up distinctly an end in itself. Be that as it may, the Scriptures affirm of a man!

The catastrophe was that that very Person was currently present, and religious men would not come to him for the life they vainly looked for in the letter of the Word (v. 40).

41-47. Jesus did not need men to have faith in him basically that he may have respect from them (v. 41). The Greek word is doxa, regularly rendered transcendence. The fundamental explanation behind the absence of reaction to him and his cases was absence of reaction to God.

They did not have the adoration for God, i.e., cherish for God. Since Jesus had come in the Father's name, this absence of adoration for God made it inconceivable for them to see that he was on with the Father, and get him. If one ought to come in his own name, not resting, as Jesus did, on the specialist of the Father, he would have a prepared reaction (v. 43).

This was likely not expected as a prediction of the happening to any one figure, however was addressed point up a standard including corrupt human instinct. The Jews were blameworthy of looking for respect and magnificence from each other (cf. 12:43) instead of from the main God, who is the main wellspring of genuine and tolerating acknowledgment.

Jesus' central goal was not one of allegation and judgment. This was pointless at any rate on account of his listeners, on the grounds that an informer existed in Moses. The Jews put unbounded trust in what Moses composed (v. 45), however at the significant point they didn't accept by any stretch of the imagination, for they neglected to get Moses' prophetic declarations with respect to the Christ.

Here we are to think not just of individual entries, for example, Deut. 18:15-18, yet of the very inadequacy of disclosure separated from One to come, and of the judgment of the Law, which required a Savior. The composed disclosure and the individual disclosure are essentially one (v. 47).

CHAPTER

SIX

The Feeding Of The Five Thousand
And
The Discourse On The Bread Of Life
(6:1-71)

A few researchers, pushing the view that parts 5 and 6 have turned out to be transposed, have brought up specific points of interest in switching them. In any case, absence of original copy confirm for it is a considerable hindrance to acknowledgment of the view.

The supernatural occurrence before us is the main "sign" recorded in every one of the four Gospels. Check and Luke talk about Jesus as instructing the hoards preceding the supernatural occurrence, yet John alone records the talk which Jesus gave on the next day.

1-4. The opposite side of the ocean, for this situation, is the eastern shore. Another name for this waterway is the Lake of Gennesaret (Luke 5:1). Pulled in by Jesus' marvels, an awesome group pursued him around the north shore.

This presupposes a service of some length, maybe a while, in the Galilean region, after the occasions of section 5 situated in Jerusalem. A mountain. The good countries. Specify of the proximity of the Passover is critical.

Since John does not record the establishment of the Lord's Supper as a piece of his presentation of the occasions of Passion Week, he is most likely drawing the consideration of the peruser to the orientation of the marvel and the talk on the focal ceremony of the Christian confidence.

5-7. The closest town was Bethsaida. It would have been troublesome for the general population to get bread, because of the separation and the delay of great importance. Jesus expected that he and his organization would make arrangement (v. 5). He advised with Philip about ways and means, knowing in himself what he would do, yet seeking to demonstrate (test) the confidence of his devotees.

Philip was a local of Bethsaida (1:44). Two hundred denarii worth of bread, the messenger assessed, would barely be sufficient. A denarius leveled with around twenty pennies and was the typical day by day wage of a worker. A worker with a normal size group of five most likely spent a large portion of his day by day wage for sustenance.

Expecting that the family ate three suppers a

day, we can presume that a half denarius would have outfitted them a day's sustenance or fifteen dinners. An entire denarius would have given two days' apportions or thirty suppers. Two hundred denarii would have given one dinner to nearly 6,000 individuals. In this group the men alone numbered around 5,000 (6:10).

8-9. It demonstrated pointless to deplete the treasury and cause troublesome deferral by trying to buy sustenance. Andrew ventured forward with data about a chap. The Greek word is utilized for an extensive variety of ages. It might show a slave additionally, however this is unlikely here. Scarcely adores. The shoddy nourishment of the average folks. The rolls were barely more than buns. The supply appeared to be pathetically little for the need.

10-11. Request was essential for the expansive operation in view. At Jesus' charge, given through the devotees, the general population were situated. Specify of grass shows the spring of the year (cf. v. 4). It made the group agreeable. Jesus then offered gratitude for the arrangement (Did he incorporate much obliged for the kid's liberality?), then circulated to the devotees, and they to the huge number.

During the time spent appropriation the marvel happened. The general population had as much as they would (longed for) both of bread and fish, as opposed to Philip's gauge "a bit."

12-13. The extravagance of the giving was coordinated by the stringency of the measures for saving what was left over. God's blessings are not to be squandered. Twelve bushel were expected to hold the sections, thus the greater part of the pupils were kept occupied.

14-15. There was undoubtedly a marvel had been performed. The general population saw it and were inspired by it. All had been profited. They saw that their advocate was no normal individual, and presumed that he should be the normal prophet (Deut. 18:18). Here, as in John 4, the prophet is by all accounts related to the Messiah, though in John 1:20-21 the two are separated.

In people in general personality there was most likely no firm line between the two representations. The prophet would get to be ruler at any rate, if this group could have its direction. Such a move would without a moment's delay express their appreciation for the supernatural occurrence and furthermore protect the saddling of Jesus' ponder working energy to the country's needs, both financial and military.

The famous desire of Messiah was going to convey what needs be in emotional design. In any case, he whose kingdom was not of this world (18:36), seeing the expectation, thwarted it by withdrawal.

16-21. The Lord who had addressed the need of the throng now addressed the issue of his pupils, who were gotten in a tempest during the evening on the lake. Without Jesus, yet obviously anticipating that him should come to them (v. 17), the followers set out toward Capernaum.

To the impair of the dull was currently included the trouble of high wind and wave. Forward advance had realized them a quarter century or thirty furlongs from the shore (each such measure-stadios-was around six hundred feet).

As the circumstance developed frantic, Jesus moved close. To the dread of the tempest was presently included the dread of the ghost. In any case, the voice of Jesus, saying, It is I; be not perplexed, exiled their feelings of trepidation. They invited him into their ship and got themselves quickly at the land.

The Synoptists reveal to us that on this event Jesus strolled on the water. His wonderful power showed itself likewise in expelling the boundary of separation. Gravity and space alike are under his control. John adds no translation to his record. The section is helpful as showing that in spite of contradicting strengths, Jesus will empower his kin to accomplish the objectives he has set for them, including paradise itself.

22-25. The setting for the talk is given in these verses. Maybe it was the tempest that shielded the general population from leaving the zone of the supernatural occurrence of the duplication of the rolls, in addition to the feeling that Jesus was still close-by.

The yearning to have him as their pioneer and supplier was still solid. Seeing that he had not left with his pupils, they were baffled as to his developments. At the point when a hunt of the region neglected to uncover him, and water crafts touched base from Capernaum, the group resolved to take dispatching and cross the lake in the trust of discovering him on the opposite side. When...? (6:25) Jesus was a man of secret to them.

26-34. Reproached by the Lord, the general population requested a sign as the reason for confidence in him. Despite the fact that they had seen the supernatural occurrence (cf. 6:14), Jesus accused them of not seeing, i.e., not looking past the outside perspective. They saw just the arrangement of material sustenance and felt its fulfillment (v. 26).

Meat (v. 27). A general word for sustenance or eating. Jesus' instructing here had a twofold edge, for he stood out nourishment that perishes from sustenance that continues unto everlasting life, and furthermore hollowed work over against give (cf. Isa. 55:1,2).

Indeed, even the nourishment Jesus had given over the lake was perishable. In any case, he had that to give which would be noteworthy for interminable life. His energy to do this rested in the specialist which God the Father had vested in him (fixed by the celestial voice at the immersion and by the bestowal of the Spirit).

The notice about work did not completely "enroll," for the general population requested to

recognize what they should do to work the works of God (v. 28), that is, to perform works worthy to him. In reply, the Lord indicated confidence as the best, the essential work (v. 29).

This appeared to be a bizarre prerequisite. All things considered, many had represented God in the past and had not called for confidence in themselves but rather just in the One who sent them. So the jam felt defended in asking for an exceptional sign to bolster this uncommon claim. To trust him they should have something much the same as the bringing down of bread from paradise (6:31), rather than the wonder over the lake.

Keeping in mind the end goal to maintain a strategic distance from mistaken assumptions, Jesus reminded his listeners that it was not Moses but rather God who gave the bread in the forsake, who additionally was allowing the genuine bread from paradise. By genuine we are to comprehend the ideal, that which answers to men's most profound need. Christ recognized the bread as he (v. 33), one who had really descended from paradise to offer life to the world.

However, the unequivocal distinguishing

proof with himself was yet not made. The general population needed this bread, however evidently still considered it in material terms, much as the lady of Samaria considered living water (v. 34).

35-65. This segment includes the talk appropriate, interfered with three circumstances by inquiries and examination.

35. Jesus now at last recognized himself as the bread of life. Does he have life in himself, as well as he can bestow it to others. In any case, this bread is not something outside, something separated from himself. One must come to him, which is what might as well be called accepting on him.

For the individuals who come, otherworldly appetite will be everlastingly ousted. Eating and drinking happen together here, maybe in suspicion of verse 53. One need never turn from Christ to another for fulfillment.

36. Seeing had not brought about trusting (cf. 6:30). "He Himself was the sign which the Jews couldn't read. No other all the more persuading could be given (Westcott, 1896).

37. All things considered, the Son was not disheartened, for all who were the endowment

of the Father to him would come, and in coming would discover in him no soul of dismissal but instead happy welcome.

38. This gathering was inescapable, for the will of the Father was the joy of the Son.

39-40. This will was not restricted to the call but rather stretched out likewise to the safeguarding of the individuals who were given to Christ (cf. 17:12). The get-together of he a day ago will challenge the force of death.

41-42. The offense of the mankind of the Nazarene blinded the listeners. They knew a lot about him, including his gathered parentage, to acknowledge the conclusion that he descended from paradise (cf. Stamp 6:2, 3).

43-44. The individuals who mumbled (as did their fathers in the betray) at the high claim of the Son of man demonstrated that they didn't recognize what it was to have the Father draw them.

Without such a drawing, a slant of the heart incited by God, one can't come to Christ. One can't shelter his own particular comprehension.

45. The drawing comes through educating as opposed to through some otherworldly procedure. Here Christ cited Isaiah 54:13. On

the off chance that the "all" be accentuated, it evacuates any component of confinement that may appear to sneak in attracting as expressed John 6:44.

46. Be that as it may, prompt learning of God can come just through the One who has seen the Father. This is a main claim of the Gospel (cf. 1:18).

47-48. Truths given before are stressed once more.

49-51. The Jews had requested that Jesus cut down bread from paradise. What perpetual benefit would come about? The fathers who ate the mana were dead, however the individuals who shared of the bread which is the Son of God would not bite the dust (profoundly), for the very existence of God was theirs. The substance of Jesus, his genuine mortal presence, was to be given for the life of the world. This indicated the cross.

52-54. As yet thinking in material terms, the Jews contended with each other over the likelihood of Jesus' giving them his tissue to eat (v. 52). Making the matter still more troublesome, our demonstrated that his blood and additionally his substance must be gotten on the off chance that one would have life (v. 53).

In perspective of the Old Testament denial against devouring blood (Lev. 7:26, 27), the offense at Jesus' words probably been increased. Those words appear to suspect the hugeness of the Lord's Supper.

55-58. The accompanying citation will best compress the idea: "The Eucharistic nourishment and drink are physically bread and wine (fellowship), profoundly the Flesh and Blood of the Son of man; the genuine sustenance and drink since they impact the sacrosanct union of the Son of God with the individuals who accept on Him, and in this manner convey endless life and certification interminability.

The union of the Father and the Son is subsequently reached out to grasp the devotees too. As the Father conveys life to the Son, so the Son imparts life to the individuals who feast upon Him, and will present on them interminability. The nourishing need not be restricted to Communion festivity.

59. A fine synagogue has been uncovered at Capernaum, which has a pot of sustenance as one of its enriching themes. Despite the fact that

this structure originates from a period later than the season of Jesus, a synagogue presumably remained on a similar spot in Jesus' day.

60-65. This area concerns particularly the response of devotees to Jesus' words. These are to be recognized alike from "the Jews" of the prior setting and the Twelve in the accompanying verses. These pupils had been supporters, however felt, in perspective of the instructing, that they couldn't proceed.

The hard saying alludes to the need of eating Christ's fragile living creature and drinking his blood. His climb, which for genuine adherents would affirm his cases, would just add to the offense for the individuals who couldn't get his mankind offered for them in death on the cross (v. 62).

Indeed, even Christ's tissue, announced to be so essential, would benefit nothing aside from as the Spirit vivified it to the adherent. His own words, notwithstanding, shared of the character of soul, that is, were nurturing. They could spare, not in freedom of notable work of the cross, however as indicating that work and translating it.

The very resistance experienced by his

words among would-be pupils exhibited that
their confidence was shallow. Jesus observed
the nearness of pesudo-confidence, as well as
the capability of treachery with respect to one
of his devotees.

66-71. The impact of the talk on the Twelve
is presently unfurled. This was the separating of
the courses for some who had been pupils (6:66).
Their takeoff provoked the subject of Jesus to
the Twelve as to their expectations (v. 67).

Subside, as the stone, persevered. His
admission is like that recorded by the Synoptists
regarding the Caesarea-Philippi episode (Matt.
16:16), however with regards to the talk it stresses
that Jesus has the expressions of unceasing life
(cf. John 6:63).

Others found in them just words. Diminish
saw a fulfillment unto life unceasing, despite
the fact that he didn't yet comprehend the cross.
Another in that organization couldn't so talk,
for he was a villain (diabolos). The significance
is not that he was an instrument of Satan when
Christ picked him, yet that he had turned out
to be such. Judas had a place with the leaving
throng, however he remained on.

Insulted that Jesus declined to be made ruler,

as we assemble from nearly concentrate his profession, he would one day deceive Him in disdain for having sold out the certainty of the individuals who put stock in Him to lead them to Messianic triumph.

CHAPTER

SEVEN

Jesus At The Feast Of Tabernacles
(7:1-53)

This chapter is completely Christ-focused as in Christ is the subject of much exchange and various response and in addition the topic of Jesus' self-revelation.

1. After these things. The reference is by all accounts to the occasions of the last part. Notwithstanding the rupture with such a large number of previous devotees, Jesus thought that it was more secure to reside in Galilee than to come back to Judea, where there was open threatening vibe.

2. The period spent in Galilee is limited by the Passover and the Feast of Tabernacles, an interim of somewhat over six months. According to the Synoptics, Jesus invested a large portion of this energy in off the beaten path places, showing his devotees.

3-9. With the approach of this harvest time devour, which drew Jews from great distances abroad for the euphoric merriments, Jesus' sibling purported to find in the event a capital open door for him to expand his impact. His supporters in Judea, maybe including numerous

Galileans who had been irritated or had developed cool in their demeanor could be won over by observing his works.

The siblings were a small scale of the immense greater part of the country, not scrutinizing the truth of the works, but rather neglecting to trust in him. Their direction was that, while Jesus was staying in mystery, he should have been known straightforwardly. This is considerably what Satan looked to recommend to our Lord in the second enticement.

Jesus' season had not arrived (somewhere else frequently called "my hour" - the season of his sign in death). The brethren had no such profound direction of their developments. They didn't know the scorn of the world, for they were a piece of it. Then again, Jesus as the Truth, needed to affirm against the malevolence on the planet.

He couldn't go to Jerusalem basically to pick up prominence. In the event that he went, it is uncover sin. I go not up yet. "Yet" is inadequate in numerous great experts, and was most likely a scribal expansion to evade inconsistency with verse 10. Jesus implied by this refusal that he was not going up on the terms proposed by his siblings. He would go time permitting and way, however would stay in Galilee until further notice.

10-13. When he went up to the devour, he went subtly, "in mystery," while the Jews (the pioneers) continued searching for him among the group and asking, "Where is that man?" The general population were talking about him likewise, with some distinction of sentiment, the judgments faltering between the decision of "good man" and "swindler." Fear of the Jews kept the discourse in quieted tones (7:13; cf. 9:22).

14-15. About the middle of the devour, i.e., amidst the week of merriments, which finished with an eighth day assembly (Lev. 23:36). Entering the Temple, Jesus started to educate. The pioneers were shocked at his articles, particularly in perspective of the way that he had not been prepared in the rabbinic schools (differentiate Paul, Acts 22:3).

16-18. Evidently it was the substance of Jesus' instructing as opposed to his way or word usage that brought about shock. Rather than gloating in his capacity, Jesus clarified that the instructing had a place with the One who had sent him, following it specifically to

God as opposed to recognizing his obligation to some human instructor as the recorders were acclimated to do.

Any individual who had the ethical point of satisfying God (doing His will) would have the capacity to figure out if Jesus' instructing was free or was a loyal generation of the heavenly. He would recognize that Jesus was not looking for his own particular transcendence but rather that of the One who sent him. Such a man would be thoughtfully pulled in to Jesus.

19-24. Jesus accused the Jews of inability to keep the Law. In this regard they were not doing the will of God. How, then, might they be able to get him whom God had sent? Their deadly aim toward him was in itself a breaking of the 6th precept.

The group, standing firm with the rulers yet not knowing their outlines, thought Jesus must be distraught, tormented by an evil spirit, to envision that his life was in risk (v. 20). It was all together for the Lord to get at the underlying foundations of the enmity of the pioneers. The one work he had done in Jerusalem that made all men "wonder" however that turned the rulers against him was the recuperating of the weak man on the Sabbath (ch. 5).

Moses himself, so painstakingly regarded by the Jews, directed circumcision (despite the fact that the practice began with the fathers and not with Moses), so it must be done on the eighth day (Lev. 12:3) regardless of the possibility that that day was the sabbath.

In this manner (John 7:22) is not by any stretch of the imagination clear as to its bearing on the matter. It conceivably indicates this line of thought - that circumcision on the Sabbath was pleasant to and really indicated such a work as Jesus had created, since the reclamation of a man both physically and profoundly was much more huge than the controlling of the indication of the pledge.

25-27. Here we experience the reflections concerning Jesus of a gathering which must be recognized from the general population of verse 20. These were occupants of Jerusalem who realized that the aim of the rulers was to murder Jesus. However the way that Jesus could talk strongly out in the open made them estimate in the matter of whether the rulers had switched themselves and were currently reasoning that this man was the Christ (v. 26).

Advance contemplation on the issue drove them to expel this plausibility, for Jesus' cause barred him from thought (cf. 6:42). The Messiah was to take care of business of puzzle no man knoweth whence he is (cf. Matt. 24:24-26).

28-31. Jesus in all actuality, as a beginning stage, that his listeners both knew him and whence he was (v. 28). However even on the natural level, they were not legitimately educated, being uninformed of his origin and probably likewise of the conditions behind his introduction to the world (cf. v. 52). They were oblivious of him in his heavenly being, and along these lines uncovered their obliviousness of God who sent him.

This censure brought a show of dismay. The men of Jerusalem were prepared to lay hands on Jesus, yet were fortunately kept from doing their plan (v. 30). Christ's hour is a reference to the time delegated by God for his passing. Some in the group were not prepared to reject the likelihood that Jesus may be the Christ. However, evidently they had confidence in him just on the premise of the supernatural occurrences and in this way were the same as prior devotees who were such just in name (cf. 2:23-25).

32-36. Continuously aware of what the man in the road was stating, the Pharisees and boss ministers (Sadducees) sent officers to catch Jesus. Such showed up again at the capture in the garden (18:3, 12). They constituted a Jewish police drive for the sanctuary territory. In the light of this advancement, Jesus demanded that his short time (cf. 16:16) was not directed by human plots against him but rather by the culmination of his work and his arrival to the Father (v. 33).

The scan of the general population for him then would be unproductive. Time was running out for them to look for him aright. "Scattered among the Gentiles." Literally, the scattering of the Greeks. It likely means the scattering of the Jews among the Greeks, making conceivable a coming to of Greeks themselves in the Jewish synagogues. This is precisely what Jesus did through his Church in later circumstances; so the announcement is unwittingly prophetic (cf. 11:52).

37-39. On the last day.... of the devour. This

could have been the seventh day or the eighth. The last was a sort of aide to the devour and furthermore a conclusion to the year's cycle of galas. On the off chance that Jesus' reference to thirst is intentionally associated with the clerics' routine of getting water a brilliant pitcher every day from the pool of Siloam and spilling it out at the holy place, then Jesus' cry of welcome would have exceptional point on the eighth day, when it appears, this service was precluded.

The thirst of the wild excursion had its supernaturally provided fulfillment, yet it repeated. Jesus offered enduring profound fulfillment (cf. 4:14). Again Judaism was uncovered as deficient. The idea advances; for the devotee to Jesus, who discovers this fulfillment, gets to be thusly a method for gift to others as a conductor of waterways of living water (7:38).

Any reference to Christ himself (cf. 19:34) is dicey. the sacred writing can't be distinguished. Some conceivable entries are Exod. 17:6; Isa. 44:3, 4; 58:11; Ezek. 47:1-9; Zech. 14:8. An option is that John has reference to no Scripture entry however to the accord of a few.

The guarantee of new life in wealth is

credited here to the Spirit, who is given to all who accept. Be that as it may, right now the Spirit had not come in the epochal feeling of Pentecost (cf. 14:26; 15:26; 16:7). Celebrated, i.e., achieved the objective of his main goal in death, revival and rising. It is the celebrated Christ whom the Spirit intercedes to men.

40-44. The uproarious cry and the way of the expressions of Jesus drove a large portion of his listeners to recognize him with the prophet who ought to come (Deut. 18:15; Jn. 1:21; 6:14). Others were set up to consider him the Messiah. This raised the issue of his cause. To meet the prerequisite of Scripture, Messiah needed to originate from David's seed and from David's town, Bethlehem.

The general population, in their numbness, considered Jesus basically a Galilean. The individuals who looked on him as an actor and swindler were supportive of laying hands on him, yet were fortunately limited (7:44).

45-49. The officers who had beforehand been sent to take Jesus (v. 32) now detailed back with practically nothing. They, similar to others (vv. 30, 44), were limited from laying hands on the Son of God, and they could clarify their disappointment just on the ground that no man ever talked as he did. They detected something otherworldly in him and were weak to complete their bonus.

The appropriate response of the Pharisees is that such men should get their direction from their bosses. So far the rulers (individuals from the Sanhedrin) and the Pharisees (instructors of the general population) had kept up a strong front against Jesus. Have any of the rulers..... believed? This stayed genuine, yet not for long, since one of the rulers was going to pronounce for Jesus, or if nothing else shield him.

The Pharisees looked to clarify mainstream enthusiasm for Jesus on the ground that the general population were oblivious of the Law and were along these lines reviled (cf. Deut. 28:15). Jewish sources showed that there was regularly awful feeling between the Pharisees and the am-ares or individuals of the land.

50-51. However well the Pharisees knew the Law, they were not submitting to it themselves, as Nicodemus had the valor to bring up. They had looked to capture a man disregarding the Law, which required that a man be heard before he could be secured in this design (Deut. 1:16).

So the Jews were unfaithful to their own Law, on which they prided themselves (cf. v. 19). Overlooking the presentation by Nicodemus, the Pharisees engaged sectionalism even as they had recently spoke to class. Nicodemus had dared to talk with regards to a Galilean, just as he were on himself. What had a Galilean to offer? It had created no prophet. In this way barring Jesus from the positions of the prophets, the Pharisees uncovered their own obliviousness, for Jonah in any event had originated from this segment (II Kings 14:25; cf. Josh. 19:13).

CHAPTER

EIGHT

The Woman Taken In Adultery
(8:1-11)

Original copy expert is emphatically against the validity of this passage (counting 7:53), and the dialect is scarcely Johannine. However the story is obviously a genuine one, which early found a place in the content of the Fourth Gospel.

1. At the point when in Jerusalem Jesus as a rule bivouacked on the Mount of Olives.

2. As a fellow he had gone to the Temple to be educated (Luke 2:46). Presently he was there to instruct, with individuals gathering around him.

3. The showing session was hindered by the landing of copyists and Pharisees, who were driving a lady secured in infidelity. Rankled at Jesus' prosperity and disappointed by their powerlessness to dispose of him, these pioneers now seized on a chance to humiliate him before the general population. they humiliated the lady, as well, by putting her in the middle.

Helping Jesus to remember the prerequisite of stoning for this offense (Deut. 22:23-24), these pioneers looked for his decision on the matter.

They were enticing him by placing him in an issue. On the off chance that he maintained the Law, which was obviously not being connected thoroughly in such cases, he could be made to seem inhumane.

On the off chance that he upheld benevolence, he could be proclaimed as having excessively indulgent a perspective of the use of the Law. On the off chance that the Pharisees had been genuinely worried for the support of the Law, they would have brought the male guilty party moreover.

6. It is pointless to guess with respect to what Jesus composed. Nothing is made of the writing in the story. Just what the gathering got notification from him (v. 9) is critical.

7. Without wrongdoing. Not really the wrongdoing being referred to, but rather sin all in all. 9. Jesus' words had the impact of moving consideration from himself and the lady to the informers.

Inner voice started to do its work. Starting at the eldest. The age made them pioneers, and their more drawn out understanding of wrongdoing gave them more prominent reason for self allegation. Just two remained - the delinquent and the Friend of miscreants. Jesus could have thrown the stone, for he was righteous; however he was more worried with the recovery of the heathen than with seeing that the Law was fastidiously fulfilled.

In the event that his statement, Neither do I censure thee, sounds excessively merciful, it is adjusted by the continuation, Go, and sin no more. The Searcher of Hearts saw that there was humility in the heart of the lady. Every one of that was required was a notice for what's to come.

Jesus' Self – Disclosure (8:12-59)

In favor of Jesus' rivals there was the question, "Who are you?" (v. 25), which is the enduring inquiry. From Christ's own angle he was the light of the world, yet One who was not of this world, the One who had come to set men free from their wrongdoings, the endless "I AM." At each point he remained in sharp differentiation to his objectors. The physical setting was still the Temple (v. 20).

12. I am the light of the world. The foundation of this announcement may live in

the act of lighting the candelabra in the Court of the Women (where the treasury was found, v. 20) amid the Feast of Tabernacles, and in the wonderfulness billow of the wild wanderings which those lights were planned to speak to, and furthermore in the creation light (1:4; 9), now imagined in otherworldly terms. He is the light of life.

13-16. Prepared to discover blame, the Pharisees protested such self-declaration and named it untrue (v. 13). Self-declaration is frequently untrue and along these lines needs bolster from others; yet for Jesus' situation, his observer to himself was valid, for he had total learning of his own beginning and fate.

Actually there was no human witness who could support such matters (v. 14). the Pharisees judged (i.e., went to a conclusion) on unimportant carnal contemplations. They were blinded to otherworldly truth (cf. I Cor. 2:14). Then again when Jesus judges (however he didn't seek that reason basically cf. John 3:17), it is appropriately a decision, thus can stand unceasingly, for it is valid.

The Father supports it and partakes in it (v. 16). On the off chance that the declaration of two men is valid (the Law required no less than two observers as a shield of equity; Deut. 17:6), the amount more legitimate is the observer of Christ, who has the Father as observer alongside himself (John 7:18). The observer of the Father at Christ's submersion and transfiguration are outstanding components of the Synoptic record.

19-20. Where is thy Father? As such, If he is a truant, we can't benefit from his witness. This is "a preeminent detailing of Jewish misconception and unbelief" (Hoskyns, 1940). Really, inability to see the genuine way of Christ was an admission of obliviousness of his Father (cf. 14:7, 9). Contact flared once more, however yet again Jesus was untouched, in light of the fact that his course had not been finished (v. 20).

21-22. The happening to his hour would mean for Jesus that he could go his way (back to The Father), yet not until he ought to have managed the wrongdoing issue. Since the Pharisees would not acknowledge him, they would need to kick the bucket in their transgressions.

Their division would be extended and fixed. They couldn't come where he would be at that day. As Jesus' expectation of his takeoff had beforehand brought about perplexity (7:35), so this time it prompted to the infer that he was considering suicide (v. 22). His demise, be that as it may, would not act naturally perpetrated; these men would achieve it.

23. The possibility of extreme division centered consideration around present complexities: beneath.....above; of this world.... not of this world. Jesus declined to talk about paradise as "that world," for the expression "world" here underlines man in rebellion and separation from God.

24. The wrongdoing which represented their obliviousness and threatening vibe woould lead them to a miserable demise unless - they put stock in him as the "I AM" (cf. Exod. 3:14).

25. This was more regrettable, from the Jews' perspective, than the claim of verse 12, for it was the supreme claim of divinity. Christ's listeners requested that he outfit a predicate. Who craftsmanship thou? Since he had made himself adequately known, he was substance to lay on his past assertions.

The Greek may conceivably imply that from the earliest starting point he was all that he had been attesting (cf. 1:1).

26. The numerous things he may have said

further would all have been valid, yet they would just have added to the judgment of their listeners (cf. the numerous things which Jesus could state to the pupils, which would just add to their perplexity; 16:12). However resistance would not close the mouth of Jesus. He would keep on speaking to the world.

28. The passing of the Son of man, his lifting up on the cross (cf. 3:14; 12;32) would vindicate him as in it would prompt to revival and commendation, which thus would bring the sentencing for the Spirit. Some at any rate, would come to realize that his claim that he was the Eternal had not been inactively spoken (Acts 2:41; 4:4; 6:7).

30-32. The cases of Jesus, so straightforward thus grandiose, awed some of the individuals who were available. Many accepted. However a little while later they were grabbing stones to cast at him (8:59). It is the old story of pseudo confidence. For this situation, they didn't reside in his pledge - which is important for genuine discipleship, and which opens the best approach to knowing reality all the more completely - to the point of being sans set through it (v. 32). These conservative articulations are opened up in what takes after.

33. The Jews despised the suggestion that they were not free. As Abraham's seed they had a standing better than that of whatever other individuals (cf. Lady. 4:22). They were children of the sublime King. They overlooked, for this situation, their political subjugation to Rome, as being unessential.

34. Their subjugation lay further than the outer relations of life. The conferring of transgression places on in the position of being the hireling of wrongdoing.

35. The Son (Christ) resides in the place of the Father for ever as the genuine Isaac. Ishmael, however he be Abraham's seed, must go out. So with the haughty Jews.

36. Reality which makes free (8:32) is currently observed to obe individual. The Son, who is reality (14:6), makes men free (cf. Lady. 4:4-7).

37. The Lord was ready to surrender that his listeners were the seed of Abraham in the conventional sense. In any case, their opposition to him demonstrated that they were not profoundly much the same as Abraham, who was a man of confidence and submission.

38. Their motivation originated from a father

other than Abraham, one whose vile personality Christ soon pronounced.

39. Abraham's youngsters ought to have the capacity to create Abraham's works. He followed up on divine revelation.

40. Christ had talked reality (not just reality about his central goal). Rather than accepting it, as Abraham would have done, these Jews tried to murder the Son of man.

41. They had a father, whom they imitated, whose works they duplicated, yet it was not Abraham. The Jews countered by a star: "We be not conceived of sex." The we is empathic. Basic this is obviously the charge of wrongness leveled at Jesus (this same charge hues Matthew's report of the introduction of Jesus).

We, the Jews were stating, are the individuals who really have God for our Father, whatever your cases might be. We backpedal of Abraham to God himself.

42. Jesus disproved the claim by the straightforward truth that their disposition toward him was not one of adoration, of family friendship. He knew he had originated from God, regardless of what they may think.

43-44. The genuine explanation behind

their inability to get him was their family relationship with the demon. He was their dad. No big surprise they went about as he does (cf. Matt. 23:15). His uncommon sins are lying (found regarding the allurement in the garden) and murder (in the impelling of Cain to kill his sibling - I John 3:12).

45-46. Since they were of the demon, the liar, they would not acknowledge reality from Christ. However they couldn't convict him of transgression. That being along these lines, they ought to have acknowledged his declaration.

47. The very inability to acknowledge his assertion fixed the way that they were not of God.

48. Stinging under a progression of censures, the Jews struck back by calling Jesus a Samaritan, i.e., one not deserving of being known as an individual from the general population of God despite the fact that he lived on Israelitish region. A more profound note might be struck here if the plan is to rehash the slur about the introduction of Jesus.

The Samaritans were blended stock, conceived of the coexisting of Israelites and nonnatives. Trying to represent Jesus' solid upheavals against them (cf. v. 52), the Jews accused him of having a villain (evil spirit).

49-50. Jesus denied the charge. To state such a mind-bending concept as this about him was sheer scorn, a shaming of him which would be brought into judgment by the Father.

51-52. Swinging to another claim, Jesus guaranteed deathlessness for the individuals who might keep his statement. This prompted to deride from the Jews, who translated his statement physically. They realized that passing had asserted the general population of God, even Abraham.

53-58. Did Jesus envision that he was more prominent than Abraham and the prophets? The appropriate response is twofold. Abraham realized that Another more noteworthy than himself was to come. He saw Christ's day (was this knowledge not given most obviously at the offering of Isaac? See Romans 8:32).

Did this imply Jesus had seen Abraham? The Jews dismisses this as crazy, for Jesus was a man in center life, and no more (John 8:57). This prompted to the second awesome claim of Jesus regarding his connection to Abraham. Before Abraham was, I am (cf. v. 24). Abraham was not at the outset with God.

59. Such statements seemed like irreverent. At the end of the day stones were ready to end such claims, however again the Lord evaded his rivals and went his direction.

CHAPTER
NINE

A Question Of Blindness:
Restoration Of A Man Born Blind
(9:1-41)

This segment has afinity with 8:12, until further notice Christ's claim that he was the light of the world got show. It additionally has close association with the accompanying part, for 10:21 shows something of the impression made by this marvel.

1-7. The performing of the sign. Jesus saw the man; then the devotees got some information about him. The enthusiasm of Jesus revived theirs, yet from an alternate point of view. To the pupils the visually impaired man was the event for religious hypothesis; to Jesus he was a person to be felt sorry for and made a difference.

The subject of the supporters (v. 2) was grounded in the conviction that substantial illness or enduring was because of transgression, regardless of whether of guardians (Exod. 20:5) or of the man himself, apparently on the premise of the spirit's pre-presence, which a few Jews held.

Jesus rejected the possibility of any uncommon sin with respect to the man or his folks and welcomed thought of a completely extraordinary approach. God had allowed this condition to exhibit His radiance, as His energy would get to be distinctly agent for this situation (v. 3).

Jesus called the followers from sit without moving hypothesis to activity. The ideal opportunity for work (day) was very short. In the better original copies the content understands, we should work. The Master was connecting their work and in addition his, despite the fact that he did it unaided (v. 4). The idea suspects 14:12. Jesus now rehashed the great claim of 8:12, as if to apply this truth to the supernatural occurrence going to be performed (v. 5).

Blessing the eyes of the visually impaired man with earth was a bit much for the cure, but rather it served to put the man's confidence to an extreme test. Would he comply? (cf. Naaman's mending) John proposes a typical essentialness for the sake of the pool - Siloam (sent). Probably the name started due to the "sending" or issuing of the waters from the spring into the pool.

In the current situation this name bears a higher sense, indicating Christ as the one sent of the Father, a truth more than once put forward in this Gospel. Submission issued in the endowment of sight (v. 7).

8-12. Neighbors and passers-by accumulated around the reestablished man. The person who sat and asked - a characteristic occupation for one so beset - now looked so changed that he made an issue of ID. Who was he? His own particular certification of personality settled the exchange (v. 9).

The following inquiry, normally, concerned the way of the cure. Opposing allurement to develop the story, the recent visually impaired man rehashed the means reliably. The third question was similarly inescapable. Who had blessed the eyes and offered order to wash? Here no answer could be given (cf. 5:13). All the more light was to come in this matter (vv. 35-38).

13-17. The gathering just specified chose it had an obligation to perform, in particular, to take the man to the Pharisees, as a result of the remarkable way of what had happened. Moreover, the cure had occurred on the sabbath day (v. 14). Afresh the man was obliged to give a record of the marvel.

His report was briefer this time, maybe demonstrating that he was losing tolerance at being investigated so much (9:15). The report made division (schisma) among these religious pioneers, who were without a doubt meeting casually. This component is noticeable in John, particularly that more profound cleavage, noted so frequently, amongst confidence and unbelief (1:11, 12; 3:36, and so forth.).

One gathering could see nothing past the way that the Sabbath had been broken. Others among them experienced issues in presuming that a heathen could finish such things. In any case, their voices did not win. Still, to redirect consideration from their own particular perplexity, the Pharisees started scrutinizing the man himself.

What did he think about his supporter? He indicated more wisdom than the pioneers. Without a doubt his companion could be no not as much as a prophet (v. 17). For sure he was that, a prophet compelling in deed (here) and furthermore in word (4:19; cf. Luke 24:19).

18-23. Rather than Pharisees, Jews are specified here, most likely not as signifying an alternate body, but rather as stressing their official position and their antagonistic vibe to Jesus (as regularly in this Gospel).

These men figured that God would not have allowed a supernatural occurrence on the Sabbath, so there more likely than not been something not right with the man's record.

They thought it is insightful to check with his folks (9:18). The guardians were certain on two matters: this was their child; he had been conceived dazzle. They could dare to concur additionally that he was currently ready to see, since the Jews had said this themselves. In any case, past this they declined to go, despite the fact that they may have known the methods if not the who of the supernatural occurrence (v. 21).

Fear made them rest all duty with their child to express the case. It was evidently basic information that the Jews (rulers) had chosen before this opportunity to suspend any individual who recognized Jesus as the Christ, i.e., the guaranteed Messiah.

24-34. The man who had picked up his sight was reviewed for further addressing. Give God the acclaim (grandness). That is, give us reality. See Josh. 7:19. Be that as it may, their opening words uncovered that they were not directing an examination. Their psyches were fixed.

They would have liked to break the man's declaration. Not able to disclaim the supernatural occurrence, they endured in viewing Jesus as a delinquent. Rather than going into level headed discussion - some time recently, he had countered the accuse of heathen of his own gauge that Jesus was a prophet - the cured man swung to safe ground, his own particular experience.

Here he could state, I know. When daze, he was presently ready to see. Others could affirm of him similar things - guardians, neighbors, companions - however the announcement was much more significant originating from his lips. The Jews' certification of learning was grandiloquence, an ex cathedra articulation; this current man's admission had the heaviness of straightforward truth behind it.

Pitifully Jews backpedaled over a similar ground about the methods by which the marvel was performed (v. 26).

Detecting that the reason for the scrutinizing was not to take in the actualities, the man got to be distinctly fretful. Why did they need a moment articulation when they didn't acknowledge the principal (v. 27)? Altogether sickened, he started to do some needling of his own. Will ye likewise be his pupils?

Presently the Jews started to fall back on verbal mishandle, blaming the man for being Jesus' pupil, something he had not avowed by any means. Moses had given the Sabbath law, and they were remaining under his standard. Jesus was a gatecrasher, a disturber of the religious peace. The main problem was the recognition of the Law versus the flexibility of Christ's administration.

In the event that the Jews had perused all of Moses and read him aright, they would not have rejected Jesus (cf. 5:45). As it seemed to be, they unflinchingly declined to trust that God had talked through him (9:29). He was an upstart. This state of mind appeared to be absurd to the man conceived dazzle. It was sublime (exceptional, stunning) that such men, who a couple of minutes before were so unquestionably saying, we know, did not know whence Jesus was-a man who had accomplished something prominent.

Where, then, was their dependability in religious matters? From the Jews themselves, without a doubt, he had heard the point which now he tossed back at them, that God would not hear heathens. The contention was sound. Caught accordingly of their own cross examinations, the Jews turned to denunciation.

The man's previous condition of visual impairment demonstrated that he had been conceived in sins (cf. 9:2) and was unfit to show them. when they cast him out, they didn't formally banish him, but instead ousted him from their nearness, which may have prompted to ejection from the synagogue later. The man had not admitted Jesus as the Christ, but rather just that he was of God.

35-41. Jesus, who first observed the man in his visually impaired condition, then mended him, now discovered him (cf. 5:14). The pariahs met - Jesus, the one cast out much sooner, and the man who had been so disappointed by his involvement with the pioneers of his kin.

Be that as it may, the meeting was not with the end goal of common sympathy. Dost thou accept on the Son of God? This was both a test to confidence and an attestation of divinity. A portion of the best original copies read Son of man here, which does not tangibly change the sense, since this indicates the man from paradise (cf. 3:13).

The question found the heart of the man open and prepared to accept. He basically requested recognizable proof of the One sent from God. It was the ideal opportunity for the self-divulgence, much as on account of the lady of Samaria (4:26). This time the man's utilization of Lord was positively more significant.

He had however of his supporter as an admirer of God (v. 31), now he was set up to love Him (v. 38). This was much more than regard to an extraordinary man; it was religious love. the scene does not close without highlighting the division made by Jesus.

One saw the light of day and passed on to see the more noteworthy learning of otherworldly things, were by and by visually impaired, and their contact with Christ fixed that visual impairment (v. 39). The brag, we see, since it accepted a shrewdness that included confidence in the Son of God, added up to an admission of visual deficiency because of the transgression of ignoring him who was the light of the world.

CHAPTER

TEN

A Commentary: The Gospel According to John

Jesus Christ, The Good Shepherd
(10:1-42)

The setting is still Jerusalem. An association between the introduction of Christ as the "Great Shepherd" and the occasions of the previous section is promptly seen. The Pharisees, acting like workers, had no genuine sympathy toward the sheep, as confirm by their state of mind toward the visually impaired man. At the point when this one had been thrown out, Jesus came and invited him into His overlap.

1-6. The educating here is known as a "story" (v. 6), however the word contrasts from the typical term. It signifies a more interesting methods of expression. Here Jesus was laying the foundation for the utilization of the figure to himself in the area which takes after.

1. Sheepfold. A nook where the sheep were protected for the night, more often than not connecting the house. It had a straightforward entryway. One bowed on theft would attempt to climb the divider.

2-3. The person who monitored the entryway was the doorman, rather than the shepherd, who picked up induction from the watchman. There is just a single shepherd here. Christ has no opponent, however there are undershepherds in his Church. His own enthusiasm for the sheep is authenticated by his calling them "by name" (cf. 1:43).

The nearness of other sheep is recommended. Not every one of those were numbered among the general population of God in that time could be known as the "Master's Sheep." "Leadeth them out" - rather than the demonstration of the Pharisees in ousting the man conceived daze.

Trust in the shepherd depends on the "voice," which uncovers the individual (cf. Gen. 27:22). No more odd can get the flick to tail him, regardless of the possibility that he prevails with regards to moving up into the overlap.

6. Jesus' group of onlookers did not get the import of his instructing (cf. 9:41).

7-18. The Lord clarified the figure as far as his own individual and mission.

7. The fact of the matter is more noteworthy than the structures through which it is passed on. In actuality, the shepherd couldn't be related to the "entryway." But the however is excessively profitable, making it impossible to let slip (cf. 14:6).

8. "All that ever preceded me." This is not a reference to sacred men of the old agreement, yet to the Jewish pioneers who had picked up a hang on the country before he raised his voice. "Hoodlums" are the individuals who basically take. "Looters" are the individuals who additionally confer savagery (cf. Matt. 23:25). "The sheep did not hear them." An a valid example was the visually impaired man, who had handed far from these pioneers over appall.

9. Did Jesus allude to undershepherds of the rush or to all devotees? Good to the previous perspective is the way that entering in has as of now been utilized of the shepherd (vv. 1, 2). Further, "to go in and out" is a commonplace Old Testament expression for the movement of a pioneer (I Sam. 18:16; II Sam. 3:25).

By the by, the expansiveness of the dialect - any man - and the words "should be spared" support a comprehensive reference. In a redemptive sense the word spare happens occasionally in John (3:17; 5:34; 12:47). The opportunity of the devotee, rather than his circumstance in Judaism, appears indicated at in going in and out, and his new fulfillment (might discover field) was a much needed development from the aridity of the instructing to which he had been subjected.

10. The work of the Good Shepherd is valuable. "Life" answers to being spared (v. 9), and plenitude answers to discovering field. Nothing in the first warrants the expansion of additional in the interpretation.

11. Here the focal disclosure in this entire example of believed is given. As the "great shepherd," Jesus satisfied the Old Testament representation of Jehovah (Ps. 23:1; Isa. 40:11), and furthermore set himself over against the pioneers who harmed the rush since they were malicious in heart.

Rather than taking life, this Shepherd was set up to give his life for the sheep. It is a prescience and also a state of mind (cf. 9:17).

12. Of an alternate sort is "the worker," who tends to the sheep and deserts them in an emergency. To some degree this photo mirrors the unfaithful shepherds (pioneers) of OT days as they are reprimanded in the prophets (see Ezek. 34).

14. The care of the Shepherd is bound up with the commonality of learning and warmth

that describes the connection amongst him and the sheep.

15. An obligation of learning exists likewise between the Shepherd and the Father who sent him. The Son knows the will of the Father (which incorporates the setting down of the life of the Son for the sheep), and the Father knows the Son, and therefore realize that he can depend on his acquiescence in doing this expensive mission.

16. "Overlap." a similar word is rendered sheepfold in 9:1. "Other sheep I have." The dialect is sovereign and prophetic (cf. Acts 18:10). Not of this overlay. Is the reference to the Jews of the Dispersion? Barely, for they were essentially one with the Palestinian Jews.

Jesus imagined the Gentiles who might react to the Gospel. "One overlap." This is not an indistinguishable word from utilized above and is appropriately rendered run (cf. one Lord, one body in Eph. 4:4, 5).

17-18. The Father adores the Son constantly (17:24), however he has an uncommon explanation behind cherishing him as a result of his dutifulness unto demise. The demise was a precept of the Father (cf. the "must" of 3:14;

Matt. 16:21). No man could touch the Son until his hour had come (19:11). "He" would convey up his soul to God (19:30). In any case, passing would not be the end. With an equivalent sway of charge, the Son would turn around the sentence of death and take up his life once more. He could certainly anticipate his revival.

19-21. For the third time in this Gospel we read of division (schisma) made by Jesus among his listeners (cf. 7:43; 9:16). Many needed to expel the Lord as disparaged and unworthy of being tuned in to. Others were inspired by the "words" he talked (without a doubt his commitment for the sheep) consolidated with the memory of the supernatural occurrence performed on the visually impaired man.

22-30. Encourage Discussion over the Identity of Jesus. Most likely an interim of around two months isolated this event from the first. The Feast of Tabernacles had a place with the fall of the year, and the Feast of the Dedication came in the winter.

This festival memorialized the purging and rededication of the blasphemy conferred by Antiochus Epiphanes. It was 165 B.C. Jesus was addressed by a portion of the Jews as he strolled in Solomon's patio, situated in the eastern segment of the Court of the Gentiles, the biggest court in the Temple region, which encompassed the inward courts and the sanctuary appropriate.

Their testing was immediate. "Make us to question." Literally, "lift up our spirit." at the end of the day, Jesus was keeping them in tension. They needed a straight answer. Is it safe to say that he was the Christ or not?

Our Lord put his finger on the trouble. It was not absence of data but rather absence of willingless to accept. His own particular declaration ought to have been adequate; if not, for their situation, then his works had an observer to tolerate for him (cf. 14:11). There was no absence of clarity for his situation; the inconvenience lay with them.

Clearly they didn't have a place with him, since they had not been willing to tail him. They saw that his shepherd educating implied another request, and they were not set up to leave the Judaism they knew, to which they clung.

However the new request offered gift and security which they couldn't have known in their Phariaism. Christ offered "endless life" as a blessing (10:28; cf. v. 10). In saying that they ought to never die on the off chance that they had a place with his sheep, Jesus utilized the most grounded type of proclamation known to the dialect.

This assurance was conceivable in light of the fact that the life offered was grounded in his blessing (Rom. 11:29) instead of in human accomplishment. His own sheep are sheltered from outsider impacts - neither might any man cull them out of my hand. The sheep have a place with Christ since they are the Father's blessing to him (10:29).

Normally the Father's has a stake in their safeguarding. Since he is incomparable - more prominent than all - it is incomprehensible that any power will have the capacity to grab them far from his defensive hand (cf. Rom. 8:38, 39). The finish of the matter is that no partition can be made between the Father and the Son.

They are more than colleagues; they are one generally (one" is not manly - one individual - but rather fix, unity of being).

31-33. For the second time Jesus was menaced with stoning by his rivals (cf. 8:59). The incitement here was his claim of unity with the Father, adding up to obscenity according to the Jews, who denied Jesus' grand source. In meeting their restriction, the Lord did not rely on upon redundancy of his claim or development on it, however turned his words to his works.

They were the less demanding to comprehend and appreciate. "Numerous acts of kindness." Attention had been centered around on a couple, yet these were illustrative of others which are not detailed (20:30). They were benevolent acts, as was not out of the ordinary in the event that they exuded from the "Father."

Could the Jews truly mean to stone a man in light of benevolent acts? In reply, the Jews neglected all reference to works, which they couldn't deny, and came back to the issue of Jesus' words, which they felt bound to preclude on the ground from securing irreverence. To them Jesus was a man who had set out to make himself out to be God. On this ground they looked for his demise now, and on this ground they would look for it later (19:7).

34-38. In this impasse the one any expectation of finding a reason for further examination lay in claim to the law (there are solid composition witnesses good to the oversight of your), since the Jews acknowledged that. Law is utilized

here in the wide sense as alluding to the OT
Scriptures.

The words being referred to, Ye are divine
beings, happen in Ps. 82:6, in reference to
Hebrew judges. God's assertion had contributed
them with a specific holiness of status as
his delegates. Since the Scripture (with
extraordinary reference to the section being
referred to) couldn't be broken to empower
men to dismiss the showing, how could protest
be raised against him whom the Father had
exceptionally separate and sent into the world?

For Christ to have said not exactly to avow
that he was the Son of God would have been
to talk a lie. To certify his Sonship was not
obscenity (John 10:36). In the event that the Jews
couldn't test his verbal quiets, they could in any
event judge on the premise of the works (vv. 37,
38; cf. vv.25, 32). It ought to be conceivable to
advance through the attempts to a confidence in
the individual. This is the pushed additionally
in 20:30,31).

39-42. The rehashed declaration of unity
with the Father brought on a danger of brutality
yet again. It was the ideal opportunity for the
Lord to leave from the city. He discovered

shelter at Bethany, past Jordan, where John had once in the past sanctified through water (v. 40). Indeed, even in retirement he would he be able to stowed away. Individuals recollected what John had said in regards to him, and they could take note of the distinction between John's service, as bereft of supernatural occurrence, and that of Jesus, which was set apart by signs.

Plainly the more prominent one had come, as John had expressed. Unbelief was no longer sensible. Many put their trust in Jesus there. Their confidence tosses into dull alleviation the hardheaded unbelief of the leaders in Jerusalem.

CHAPTER

ELEVEN

The Raising Of Lazarus
(11:1-57)

John presents his readers surprisingly to three great companions of Jesus: Mary, Martha, and Lazarus. The Text reminds the perusers that it was Mary who blessed the Lord with salve and wiped his feet with her hair. This sentence at the opening of part 11 is intriguing in that John relates that very occasion in the following section (12:1-8).

There is, in this way, no reason for this distinguishing proof with the end goal of this present Gospel's story advancement, unless it is John's worry to recognize the scene in Mark's Gospel in which Mark does not give Mary's name (Mark 14:3-9).

I trust it is the most sensible presumption to perceive this reference as one more sign that John knows about the other Gospel authors, and that he makes the distinguishing proof now to help his perusers to remember Mark's record. It is likewise a confirmation of the prior composing and course of Mark.

Luke is the main other Gospel essayist who makes reference to Jesus' association with his family. Luke 10:38 recounts a visit by Jesus to the home of Mary and Martha. Along these lines John's recognizing proclamation gives us another proof of how generally flowed the Gospel records were among the early holy places.

Alternate Gospels reveal to us that amid Jesus' opportunity in Jerusalem he spent his night at Bethany, a little town over the valley Kidron and somewhere in the range of two miles from Jerusalem. It is John who tells in detail of the family with whom Jesus remained.

The name Lazarus is the abbreviated type of Eleazar, which we know is a typical name amid the main century. The raising of Lazarus is given an exceptionally unmistakable position in John yet is not said in alternate Gospels. This does not astonish us, in any case, since we have generally expected from John that he will particularly talk about occasions which alternate Gospels don't specify - i.e., the meeting with the lady at the well, the marriage at Cana, Nicodemus, the man at the pool of Bethesda, the young fellow conceived daze.

The Lazarus supernatural occurrence is depicted by John similar to the essential occasion that triggers the fierceness of Jesus' adversaries to the indicate that they concur a lethal methodology against him.

John here establishes a noteworthy bit of the mental confound; that is, the manner by which this instructor from Galilee could turn out to be so celebrated with the general population to motivate the general population show of warmth on Palm Sunday and after that, how such solid restriction could have combine to the point of assention among fundamentally different gatherings like the Sadducees and the Pharisees.

This record incorporates the account of the infection, demise, and restoration of Jesus' companion and the response of authority Judaism to the wonder. It finishes up with a notice of the increased well known enthusiasm for this man who was mixing the country. The One who had substantiated himself the "Light of the world" by offering sight to the visually impaired man now showed himself as the "Light of men," the "Overcomer of death."

1-4. John gives the setting for the wonder - the ailment of Lazarus and the correspondence of this reality to Jesus. Mary and Martha are specified just as they were at that point well known to the peruser (cf. Luke 10:38-42), yet Lazarus needs presentation since his name does not show up in the Lucan account. It is of intrigue that each of the three of these names happen on ossuary engravings of Judea exhumed as of late, demonstrating that such names were normal in this period (Allbright, 1962).

The author suspects his own particular account of 12:1-9 in recognizing Lazarus as the sibling of that Mary who blessed the Lord (11:2). In passing on the data about Lazarus' disease to Jesus, the sisters demonstrated striking restriction, being content just to express the reality, without making demand (v. 3). However the say of Jesus' adoration for Lazarus was a types of offer in itself, fragile to be sure.

This affliction is not unto demise. Indeed, even as he spoke, Lazarus was likely officially dead (cf. v. 39). The words have a place with a higher plane of significance, related with the eminence of God, which is likewise that of the Son. A revival would show that grandness (a disclosure of perfect power) more completely than rebuilding from a wiped out bed.

5-6. Jesus' affection for the whole family is

noted, just to be tested, in appearance at any rate, by his own inaction in residual where he was for two days, with no move to come back to Bethany. The last part of the section disentangles the riddle. By holding up, then coming and raising Lazarus from the dead, Jesus blended up such resistance as to make his own passing certain. This was the measure of his adoration for the family at Bethany.

7-16. Discourse between the Lord and his pupils over the Lazarus emergency. Jesus proposed an arrival to Judea - not Bethany, as if they may visit the family, then return - yet Judea, the focal point of restriction to himself. The devotees got at this promptly. It appeared to be foolhardly, such as strolling into a trap.

Jesus had scarcely gotten away from a stoning not much sooner (11:8; cf. 10:31, 39). The Master's answer may have picked up point by being talked not long after first light. It connected both to himself and to his adherents. He could wellbeing backpedal to Judea the length of he was strolling in the light of the Father's will.

His adversaries couldn't touch him until his hour had come. At that point for a concise time the dimness of profound restriction would be allowed to shut in upon him (v. 9). With respect to the pupils, it benefitted them not to stroll in the haziness of self-will and detachment from him. Without his light, they would to be sure bumble (cf. 9:4, 5).

Our companion Lazarus sleepeth. Not knowing about his demise, the devotees translated this idiom of the Lord truly and found in it ground of seek after his recuperation. However, Jesus had utilized "rest" in an uncommon sense as reference to adherents' demise (cf. Acts 7:60; I Thess. 4:13). He took after this with the limit declaration that Lazarus was dead (John 11:14).

Another Catch 22 is the Savior's colloquialism that he was happy he had not been there. The reason is clear. Had he been there, Lazarus would not have kicked the bucket (nobody ever did in His nearness); and all things considered one of the best lessons of confidence going to be urged the supporters through Lazarus' restoration would have been inconceivable (v. 15).

The supporters were never so progressed as not to need affirmation and improvement of their confidence. Thomas, called Didymus (twin), was the first to react to Jesus' second proposition to go into Judea (11:15, 16; cf. v. 7).

17-19. "Four Days." Likely Lazarus passed on not long after the emissary was sent. Permitting a day for his travel, two days of hesitating by Jesus, and one day for the arrival, we touch base at this aggregate. The separation from Bethany past Jordan to Bethany close Jerusalem was around twenty miles.

Since the sharpen was two miles from the city of Jerusalem (cf. v.18), a large portion of the Jews thought that it was conceivable to come and offer sympathies. Jews here does not allude to rulers (pioneers of the general population).

Their nearness was two-edged, be that as it may. Having come to Bethany as grievers, some of them came back to Jerusalem as witnesses (11:46).

20-27. The meeting amongst Jesus and Martha. Both sisters show up in this record in trademark parts. Martha, good to go, was the one to welcome Jesus. Mary, assimilated in her distress, sat still. Martha had one lament - Jesus had not been there. What a distinction his nearness would have made!

However she voiced no feedback. As officially noted, Lazarus was dead when the news of his ailment came to Jesus. Martha felt in Jesus a tower of quality. Her words (v. 22) practically challenge investigation, be that as it may. They are a declaration of trust in him as being in close touch with God and ready to get a shelter from him; yet quick revival does not appear to have been in her psyche (cf. v. 24).

In insisting the revival of Lazarus, Jesus did not name at whatever time (v. 23). Martha provided this - at the most recent day; however she said it without excitement, for in the mean time her sibling lay in the grasp of death. The Lord now moved to right Martha's flawed confidence (cf. v. 22) by attracting her consideration regarding his lordship over death. I am the restoration and the life.

For this situation the disclosure of word went before the disclosure of deed. The instructing goes past the instance of Lazarus and incorporates all who accept. Two truths are expressed here. The devotee may kick the bucket, as Lazarus had done, however by Christ's energy will live, i.e., encounter restoration. Be that as it may, significantly more essential is the ownership of endless life increased through confidence in Christ.

The individuals who have this life can never pass on in the feeling of being isolated from the wellspring of life (vv. 25, 26). Tested to trust this, Martha made the very admission for which this book was composed (11:27; 20:31), however she didn't comprehend the ramifications of her own announcement. To her, Christ was not yet the supreme Lord of life and passing, a total Savior (cf. vv. 39, 40).

28-32. Jesus and Mary. Martha passed on to Mary unobtrusively (subtly) the news that the Master (instructor) had come, most likely wanting to make conceivable a private meeting with Jesus for her sister. Be that as it may, the Jews who were available taken after Mary to the place outside the town where Jesus and Martha had met, for they thought at first that she was going out to go to the grave.

As token alike of respect and of her own defenselessness, Mary fell at his feet. Her opening words were the same as those of Martha. Presumably this opinion had been communicated again and again by the two after the demise of their sibling.

33-37. The pain of Jesus. He moaned in the soul. The Greek word for moaned, rehashed in verse 38, appears to be frequently to pass on the possibility of outrage regarding something. Since Christ could barely have felt outrage toward Mary and the grieving companions, it is conceivable that his profound feeling was because of his deep down dissenting the ruin sin has brought into the world, with sickness and passing (death) and distress (sorrow) as its terrible entail.

While in transit to the tomb, Jesus sobbed, breaking out into tears. This was quiet sobbing as opposed to Christ's perceptible sobbing over Jerusalem (Luke 19:41). The Jews who were available found in the sobbing a proof of Jesus' awesome friendship for Lazarus, however they found in it likewise confirmations of his constraint.

He had offered sight to the visually impaired (John 11:9), yet demise was excessively incredible for his forces (v. 37). Maybe in the second moaning there was a blending of resentment at this shallow perspective of his energy.

38-44. The Miracle. This surrender at

Bethany has been depicted by one who reviewed it in advanced circumstances as of the profound shake cut sort. Take ye away the stone. No one but Christ could raise the dead, yet others could take an interest as indicated by their capacity. Martha, stunned at such a request from Jesus, attempted to mediate a protest; she thought the body had unquestionably started to disintegrate.

Four days had passed since death. Without saying what he proposed to do, Jesus summoned Martha to confidence, helping her to remember his past words, evidently beholding back to verse 23. Be that as it may, this time he expressed the coming occasion as far as the transcendence of God (cf. 11:4).

The brilliance here was the force of God in operation, proclaiming his sway (cf. 2:11). There could be no turning back now, the stone was evacuated (v. 41). One thing more stayed to be finished. For the general population (actually, the large number) it must be clarified that what was going to be done would be done through the group of life and power delighted in by the Son with the Father - that they may accept.

This was not a demand to be heard but rather a supplication of thanksgiving for a consistent obligation of fellowship and comprehension. The hold of death was broken by the voice of expert calling, Lazarus, approach. Christ had pronounced that the time was coming when all the honorable dead would correspondingly comply with that same expert (cf. 5:28, 29).

The Lord left untouched the work of adoring hands that had arranged the body for internment, that they may have the excite of fixing that work and setting Lazarus free. (Review human support in evacuating the stone).

45-46. The wonder brought about a distinctively changing reaction. A significant number of the Jews.....believed; others went to the Pharisees to report what had occurred.

47-50. The Effect Upon The Sanhedrin. This was one of numerous marvels. The rulers felt totally baffled. What were they to do? They communicated the dread that every one of the general population would accept on him - in the feeling of giving him their support and tailing him as their Messiah.

This would positively bring the Romans down on the Jews with drive, as they would translate such an unbelievable marvel as a political unrest. At that point the Jews would lose their place (Temple) and country. Under the Romans, since the season of Julius Caesar, they had appreciated certain benefits as "the country of the Jews."

Precisely the circumstance they dreaded developed therefore of the war of the Jews against Rome, A.D. 66-70. Disgracing the gathering into quiet with his rebuff, "Ye know nothing by any stretch of the imagination," Caiaphas laid out a strategy that was heartless however straightforward: Get freed of the guilty party. Make him bite the dust for the general population, so that the entire country would not die. That year. Not reference to residency of office, but rather to the significance of that year for Israel and the world.

51-52. John needed his perusers to detect the way that this articulation of the esteemed minister was prophetic. The words, as it were, were put into his mouth. He forecasted. Here is a Balaam who might revile Jesus, however out of the prediction comes the acknowledgment of the motivation behind God that Christ ought to kick the bucket for he country in a redemptive, vicarious sense, and notwithstanding for a bigger gathering, that all the scattered offspring of God (in a planned sense) would be united (cf. 10:16).

How fitting it was that one who filled the workplace of devout cleric ought to unwittingly set forward the work of Christ as the Lamb who takes away sin!

53-54. The advice of the devout minister hardened the reason for the committee so that, from that time forward, it was completely decided on Jesus' passing. On this record Jesus thought that it was astute to resign from the region and go to a place called Ephraim, in a close abandon segment. This has been probably distinguished as a place twelve miles or so north of Bethany, close where the high level splits away in tough territory driving down to the Jordan valley.

55-57. With the current passover, Jesus couldn't be truant from the city for long. Since the time was not yet ready, Ephraim was not a viable alternative for the second story room. Jesus' next doings are shrouded peacefully. John moves our consideration regarding the travelers who started to wend their approach to Jerusalem.

Generally they were well disposed to Jesus,

rather than the specialists, and traded feelings with each other concerning whether their saint would set out to overcome the resistance of the gathering by going to the devour. There more likely than not been numerous sources if the rulers had any hold at all upon the general population (v. 57).

CHAPTER

TWELVE

Jesus In Bethany And Jerusalem
(12:1-50)

The occasions included here are: the blessing
of Jesus by Mary of Bethany (vv. 1-11); the
Triumphal Entry (vv. 12-19); the happening to
the Greeks (vv. 20-26); Jesus' awareness of the
moving toward Passion (vv. 27-36); the unbelief
of the general population and their rulers (vv. 37-
43); Jesus' last open supplication for confidence
(vv. 44-50).

The dinner at Bethany is described with
specific varieties from the records in Matthew
and Mark.

1. Six days before passover, i.e., Saturday.
Alternate records give the area as the place of
Simon the pariah. John alone says the nearness
of Lazarus.

2. They made him a dinner. Simon would
have felt appreciation for his mending, and the
sisters of Lazarus for the raising of their sibling
from the dead.

3. A pound (litra), a measure of twelve
ounces. Spikenard. Oil from a plant developed
in northern India, expensive as an import into
Palestine. Mary is constantly connected with

the feet of Jesus (Luke 10:39; John 11:32). The house was loaded with the smell of the treatment. This answers in its way to the Gospel this demonstration would be told as a dedication of the lady. The scent of the demonstration would have a wide dissemination and an enduring impact.

5. Judas assessed the estimation of the nard at three hundred pence, or about sixty dollars.

6. His clear sympathy toward the poor was a shroud for his own particular greed. He had quite recently missed a possibility for robbery on a bigger scale than normal. Apparently he didn't make a general treasurer's report.

7. Jesus protected Mary by stopping the feedback. Leave her be. It shows up from the Synoptics that Judas, stung by this reproach, slipped out and haggled with the central clerics to deceive the Master. Jesus found in Mary's demonstration a profound essentialness - against the day of my covering hath she kept this.

However much Mary may have wished to help the poor conventionally, she had held this valuable part for Christ.

She foreseen his passing. As opposed to the rulers, Mary put stock in Jesus' individual;

rather than numerous who had confidence for the most part, her confidence incorporated the work of the Savior - his demise.

9. Lazarus demonstrated a fascination in a significant number of the general population, who came to see him and in addition Jesus. These were interested yet thoughtful.

10-11. Interestingly, the main ministers found in the circumstance motivation to incorporate Lazarus in their dim plotting as one who was improving the reason for Jesus. A moment murder would not have exasperates their solidified still, small voices.

The following occurrence has turned out to be customarily known as the Triumphal Entry, albeit such a title better fits Jesus future coming.

12. Plainly the individuals who looked to respect the Lord were explorers, not occupants of Jerusalem. They had sought the galas of Passover.

13. John alone specifies the utilization of palm branches. They are refered to by the essayist of II Macabees (10:7) regarding the rededication of the Temple by Judas Macabaeus after its profaning by the Syrians. Hosanna. A Hebrew expression significance, Save, I ask (cf.

Ps. 118:25). In the New Testament its utilization is kept to this episode. Now and again it was less a supplication but rather more an attribution of acclaim, and such is its utilization here.

Jesus was being saluted as King of Israel, who had accompanied the specialist of the Lord (Jehovah). These individuals were looking to him to build up David's kingdom with power (cf. Stamp 11:10). The group was loaded with Messianic desire (cf. John 6:15).

14-15. Jesus.......found. The story is given in Mark 11:1-6. John is the main Evangelist who depicts the creature as a youthful ass (onarion). Jesus' demonstration satisfied the prophetic word (Zech. 9:9). The ass, superior to anything the stallion, symbolized the quiet and serene character of the King of Israel. This in itself pronounced that Jesus' comprehension of the occasion contrasted from that of the throng.

16. Just when Jesus was celebrated, just when the Spirit had come to teach and convey the things of Christ to their recognition (7:39; 14:26), did the supporters see this entire scene in the light of Scripture and the arrangement of God.

17-18. John educates his perusers that no little part of the eagerness shown amid the walk on Jerusalem was because of the raising of Lazarus. The general population who were with Jesus on that event exposed record (continued taking the stand). Another gathering, pioneers to the devour who had just known about the marvel, progressed to meet Jesus and hail him as their national saint.

19. This influx of fame cast down in the camp of the Pharisees. In their cynicism they proclaimed that the world (everyone concerned) had followed Jesus.

20. The development toward Jesus proceeded in the occurrence of the Greeks who communicated a yearning to see Jesus. They were delegates of the world in a bigger sense than that proposed by the Pharisees..

It was fitting that the Greeks ought to show up now, on the eve of the Passion. They would benefit from the Savior's passing, as would the colossal host of Gentiles whom they spoke to. Revere. Court of the Gentiles. Before long, in Christ, the center mass of segment would be separated. It gives the idea that these men took after Cornelius of a later time. They could be called God-fearers, however were not followers who had joined the gathering of Israel.

21. Philip is a Greek name. This follower was a characteristic purpose of contact with Jesus. See Jesus, i.e., have a meeting with him.

22. Andrew additionally is a Greek name. This supporter appeared to represent considerable authority in conveying individuals to Christ (1:41; 6:8,9).

23. Without tending to the Greeks specifically, Jesus addressed their issue. they would not need to hold up long to benefit from his main goal - the hour is come. Celebrated. This is clarified in the accompanying verse. In John's Gospel glorification starts with death and incorporates restoration.

24. Corn. Grain or seed. Nature gives a story of Jesus' profession. Aside from death his life remains in segregation, with no force of increment. Demise is the way to otherworldly productivity.

25. He that loveth his life. Similar standards gets for the pupil. "He who looks to accumulate round himself that which is perishable, so far perishes with it: he who strips himself of all that is this world just, so far sets himself up for higher life" (Westcott, 1896).

26. Give him a chance to take after.

Serving Christ includes tailing him, even unto passing. This will be remunerated by imparting the magnificent future to him, including acknowledgment by the Father. This prospect is interested in any man (Greek and additionally Jew).

27. By talking about these things, Jesus was made all the more intensely aware of the value he would soon be paying for the satisfaction of his office as Redeemer. Spare me. This is a touch of Gethsemane misery. Jesus common slant was to be spared from the hour that was moving close.

Such a supplication bears expressive declaration to the terribleness of great importance. Yet, Jesus' dedication was complete to the point that he needed to face it. That was the reason he came. So the petition was not drawn out.

28. Another supplication had its spot. Laud thy name. The Father would do this as he empowered the Son to face his hour and finish his main goal. I have ..... celebrated. The transcendence of the Son, showed in life and work up to this point, pondered greatness the name of the Father. Once more, to be specific,

in the Passion which would issue in restoration and worship.

29. The general population, constrained in their comprehension, confused the Father's witness.

31. Jesus' hour would bring languishing over him as well as judgment upon the wicked world that would put him on the cross, and demolish for Satan, who heads up the world framework. The removed Christ would oust the person who drives men to reject Him (cf. Col. 2:15).

32. Christ himself, when in position to attract men to himself by the force of his give up. Greatness would radiate through dull catastrophe. All men, the Greeks included, would come to know the draw of his reclaiming love. Unto me. Salvation is unto Christ and also through him.

33. What (kind of) death. The lifting up answers to execution. Jesus knew he would not kick the bucket by stoning.

34. The Christ (Messiah) whom the general population had figured out how to anticipate from the law (OT when all is said in done) abideth for ever. How, then, could Jesus as the Son of man satisfy this desire by being lifted

up to kick the bucket? Such a Son of man did not concur with their Messianic desires. The trusts they had engaged at Christ's entrance into Jerusalem were presently dashed.

35-36. Prior to the contact with the general population was broken, Jesus cautioned them that the light would sparkle just temporarily. In the event that they didn't get it, dimness would cover them.

The notice clearly went unnoticed. John abridges the imperviousness to the light that proceeded to the end (vv. 37-43).

37. The supernatural occurrences had not conveyed the hoards to confidence in the Lord. Just examples of the supernatural occurrences out of many are found in John.

38. This absence of confidence was in understanding of Isaiah (53:1). Fundamentally, this is the section in Isaiah that offers unmistakable quality to the passing of Messiah.

39-40. They couldn't accept. Their remorselessness made this inescapable. Blinded.... solidified. This action of God can't be seen as intentionally wanted to make confidence unthinkable for the individuals who craving to accept. Or maybe, this is the appropriate response of God to unbelief. The Lord would need to mend them on the off chance that they changed over (swung to him), so his devotion is not reproved. Legal solidifying is a period of awesome judgment. The Quotation is from Isaiah 6:10. I ought to mend. Christ turns into the subject here.

41. His wonderfulness, i.e., Christ's. Indeed, even as Isaiah anticipated His sufferings (cf. v. 38), so he saw his eminence (Isa. v. 6).

42-43. By and by readies the peruser for a special case to the for the most part solidified state of Israel. The personality of these rulers who "accepted" is obscure. Unwillingness to admit Christ, be that as it may, tosses question on the entire validity of the confidence of these men (cf. 2:23-25). They substantiated themselves unworthy of heavenly recognition.

Now John presents Jesus' last introduction of himself to the country.

44-45. Cried, underlining the general population character of the educating and its criticalness. Jesus reaffirmed his bonus from the Father (12:44) and his unity with him (v. 45)

46. A light. Cf. 1:7-9; 3:19; 8:12; 9:5; 12:35.

47-48. On the off chance that the expressions

of Christ were dismisses now, they would go about as judge in the most recent day. His words could never pass away.

49. Jesus had said just what the Father had offered him to talk. How then would he be able to be liable of lewdness or falsehood?

50. Life everlasting. This is found in the talked expression of Jesus, even as it is available in himself as the Word (6:63; 1:1,4,18).

CHAPTER

THIRTEEN

The Foot-Washing
(13:1-17)

From the Synoptics we figure out how Jesus sent two of his followers to set up the second story space for the devour and the partnership he had wanted to have with his supporters (Luke 22:7-13).

1. Presently before the devour of the passover. This brings up issues. Was the feast in the second story room a partnership dinner, or would it say it was really the Passover? In two different entries not ye come (13:29; 18:28). It is clear from the Synoptics that Jesus and the followers ate the Passover.

The references in John 13:29 and 18:28 to the Passover as still future are to be disclosed as references to the Feast of Unleavened Bread, which was once in a while called the Passover (Luke 22:1). This started promptly after Passover and proceeded for seven days. All things being equal, the dinner alluded to here appears to have been held before the Passover, regardless of whether it be viewed as a legitimate perception of the yearly devour or not.

Hour. Seen here not from the outlook of

anguish but rather of vindication and come back to the Father (cf. 19:30, Luke 23:46). Adored them unto the end. On the other hand, toward the end (at the finish of days of arrangement and suspicion). The expression (eis telos) may likewise signify "unto the most extreme" (cf. I Thess 2:16).

2. Dinner being finished. Another perusing, generally embraced in present day interpretation, yields the importance, while dinner was going on. The move made by Jesus to wash the followers' feet would have been more suitable then than later. The affection for Jesus remains in sharp complexity to the scorn of Satan and Judas.

3. Had of the information of his power, of his celestial source, and of his specific come back to the Father, Jesus did not hate to lower himself to play out a humble administration. This is the virtuoso of the soul of the Incarnation.

4-5. The materials for washing the feet were available (cf. Luke 22:10), however there was no hireling (Jesus had asked for finish protection). One of the supporters may have volunteered, however all were excessively glad. About this time they were questioning as to which of them ought to be viewed as the best (Luke 22:24).

6. It can't be resolved regardless of whether

Christ came to Peter most importantly. What is clear is Peter's feeling of the unfitness of having the Lord play out this administration on him. The pronouns "thou" and "my" are empathic. Strikingly the supporter said what he was considering.

7. In Jesus' answer there is a comparable accentuation on "I" and "thou." Now... from now on. Not a reference to paradise or to the occasions of the night, however to the illumination of the Spirit later on.

8. More awed with the evildoing of the circumstance than with its concealed significance. Diminish demanded that Jesus ought to never wash his feet. In any case, the reply of the Lord lifted the demonstration from one of modest administration to one of otherworldly hugeness. To be unwashed by Christ is to be unclean, to have no part with him.

9. The option of being sundered from Christ was far more awful to Peter than the disgrace of being served unto thusly by his prevalent. Subsequently the incautious incorporation of hands and head. Every single other part were, obviously, secured. Diminish needed nothing prohibited that could be washed.

10-11. Diminish had to realize that the excellence in the washing was not quantitative, for the demonstration was typical of internal purging. "Washed" (from louo) signifies a total body shower. "Wash"..... "feet." Here the word is nipto, fitting for washing of individual parts of the body, as in the past account.

The washing of recovery makes one clean in God's sight. This is symbolized in Christian immersion, which is regulated just once. Additionally purging of the spots of debasement is not a substitute for the underlying purifying but rather has meaning just in the light of it (cf. I John 1:9). Ye are spotless, yet not all. The reference is to Judas. Jesus "knew" his heart and his arrangement (cf. 6:70, 71). For "clean," see 15:3. Judas was an unregenerated man.

12. Know ye what I have done to you? The perfect side of the demonstration had as of now been clarified as far as purifying, however the human side should have been put forward - the go about as typical of what followers should accomplish for each other.

13-14. On the off chance that their unrivaled, the person who was Lord and Master (educator), was eager to play out this administration for them, most likely they should do it for each other. Quietude is not basically self-refusal but rather losing oneself in support of others.

15. An illustration. This guidelines out any considered foot-washing as a holy observance. Sacred writing is noiseless about the practice spare as a cherishing ministration practiced as an issue of accommodation (I Tim. 5:10).

The Announcement Of The Betrayal (13:18-30)

Judas had been on the Lord's brain notwithstanding amid the foot-washing (vv. 10,11). Presently it was difficult to keep back any more extended the divulgence to that a double-crossing would happen. In extraordinary shrewdness Jesus prevailing with regards to telling Judas that He knew about his expectations and in confining him from the organization. He in this manner gave the correct sort of climate in which to continue with His educating.

18. I talk not of all of you. Judas couldn't be relied upon to benefit by the case given in the foot-washing. I know whom I have picked - Judas included. The Scripture had pre-composed the

bad form of this man (Ps. 41:9). Not all the vers is cited, for the main half is not relevant.

19. Any enticement with respect to alternate pupils to scrutinize the shrewdness of Jesus in the selection of Judas was in this manner blocked, for Christ was not being shocked. At the point when the Passion was over, these men would have the capacity to think back and have faith in their Lord more solidly than any other time in recent memory.

20. Judas would not go forward as illustrative of Christ, but rather these men would. They bore the Savior's name and expert. The individuals who reacted would react to Christ. This rule is grounded in Jesus' own connection to the Father.

21. Jesus now uncovered to the reason for the vexed condition of his heart. A double-crosser was in the middle - "one of you."

22. Perplexity about the distinguish of the double-crosser held the biblical circle. Judas had his influence well. He was unsuspected by his colleagues.

23. The "darling follower" possessed a place quickly by Jesus at the table. He could incline toward the Savior's chest due to the leaning back position usually utilized.

24. On edge to realize who the double-crosser was, Peter, too far away to ask Jesus face to face, enticed John to ask of the Lord.

25-26. In light of the whispered question of John, Jesus recognized the deceiver, not by name but rather by demonstrating that he was the one to whom He would hand the sop, a piece given in token of extraordinary support and kinship. He gave it to Judas. Iscariot likely signifies "man of Kerioth," a town in Judea.

27. Acknowledgment of the sop without acknowledgment of the arguing love that ran with it implied that Judas was steeling his heart to do what he had contracted to do - deceive the Lord. He had been found and despised it. From this hour Satan was completely in control. "Do rapidly." Further endeavors to deter Judas were futile.

28. No man....knew. Clearly Judas was situated by Jesus, on the inverse from John. The expression of summon that rejected Judas was detached with the selling out in the brains of the others.

29. Realizing that Judas was their treasurer, they expected that he was being conveyed to make buys for further devouring or else to impart something to poor people (Neh. 8:10).

30. It was night. In a written work so delicate to imagery and hidden importance as this Gospel, these words must have exceptional criticalness. They picture on the double the ignorant state of Judas through surrender to contempt of Jesus and furthermore the happening to the hour when the forces of dimness would inundate the Savior.

The Upper Room Discourse
(13:31 – 16:33)

These valuable expression of Christ were talked in the light of his approaching flight to the Father and had in view conditions under which the Lord's devotees would need to continue without his own nearness (16:4). Three key strands of instructing are perceivable:

(1) charges concerning the errand set before the supporters, which was a fruitbearing witness undergrided and saturated with adoration; (2) notices about the restriction to be confronted from the world and from Satan; and the greater part of every one of the (3) an article of the awesome arrangements by which the devotees would be managed and made triumphant in the coming days.

Every now and then the Lord's lessons was hindered by inquiries, demonstrating that the supporters needed comprehension at many focuses.

31-35. Declaration of the flight and charge to love each other.

31. Presently is the Son of man celebrated. With the exit of Judas, the stage was quickly being set for that arrangement of occasions that would convey brilliance to the Son and to the Father. In death Christ would be celebrated according to the Father (cf. I Cor. 1:18,24). The Father would find in the passing of the cross the satisfaction of his own motivation. Simply after the Resurrection would the devotees sense the glorification.

32. God might likewise praise him in himself. In the restoration and worship of Jesus and in the spilling out of the Spirit upon the followers, God would make it show that the One who was respectful unto demise and was presently regarded for his constancy, was unified with himself, even as he had guaranteed.

33. Little kids. Delicate fondness is honed by the impact of goodbye. The Jews may search him to straighten something up, and his own

particular out of individual connection; in either case, be that as it may, it would be vain for them to look for him in any physical sense.

34. There was something, be that as it may, to which they could appropriately dedicate their energies. Another commandment...love each other. It was new in that the adoration was to be practiced toward others not on the grounds that they had a place with a similar country, but rather on the grounds that they had a place with Christ.

Furthermore, it was new in light of the fact that it was to be the declaration of the consummate love of Christ, which the supporters had found in life and would see likewise in death. As I have cherished you was immediately the standard and the rationale force of the affection that should have been showed.

35. Such love would definitely be a declaration to the world. It would sustain the recognition of Christ and indicate his proceeding with life, for this nature of affection has been seen just in him. Men perceive the blessedness of such love despite the fact that they can't of themselves create it.

36-38. Dwindle declined to acknowledge the

possibility of division. He was informed that he couldn't take after Christ then, however he could a short time later (cf. John 21:19).

Prepared to take after now, Peter was set up to surrender his life for his Lord. Such confidence required a miserable censure. Subside's proposed steadfastness was to issue in base foreswearing, thrice dedicated.

CHAPTER

FOURTEEN

Specific Encouragements To Counterbalance Jesus' Departure, The Defection Of Judas, And The Predicted Failure Of Peter (14:1-31)

In reference to the title the supportive gestures to balance are: a definitive arrangement of the Father's home; the arrival of Christ for his own; the possibility of doing more prominent works; boundless petition plausibility; the endowment of the Holy Spirit; and the arrangements of Christ's tranquility.

1. In the event that Peter, the pioneer of the missional gathering, would fall flat, it is no big surprise hearts were vexed. This word is utilized of Jesus himself in John 11:33; 12:27; 13:21. "He shared the encounters which in us He would solace and control (Bernard, 1892, 2012)."

"Accept" is most likely a basic in both cases. Everything appeared very nearly crumple. A reestablished confidence in God was essential. The reason for Jesus appeared to be confronted with annihilation; so confidence in him was more needful than any other time in recent memory. Each crisp test and in addition each new disclosure is a summons to confidence.

2. My Father's home (cf. 2:16). The Temple at Jerusalem, with its limitless courts and various chambers, proposes the antitype in paradise. Numerous houses. Spots of residence. An indistinguishable word from in 14:23. I would have let you know. The follower is justified in expecting a satisfactory perfect arrangement notwithstanding when it is not expressed. I go to get ready. As Peter and John had proceeded to set up the chamber for the dinner, so Jesus was going before the rest into eminence to set up "the second story room" for his own.

3. I will come back once more. Linguistically, this is a modern present, accentuating both the conviction of the coming and the approaching way of the occasion. The coming does not accentuate paradise accordingly yet rather the get-together of Christ and his kin.

Where I am - the most fulfilling meaning of paradise. This apatial dialect makes it hard to translate the verse as an arrangement for Christ's proceeding with nearness with his kin while they are on earth. The utilization of the words to the passing of the devotee is insufficient likewise, for in that experience the holy people of God leave to be with Christ (Phil. 1:23).

4. The best content yields the rendering, And where I am going ye know the way.

5. Thomas saw a twofold issue in Jesus' articulation. Since he, and additionally others, didn't comprehend the goal, how might he know the way?

6. The Way. This has exceptional conspicuousness on account of the specific situation. It had been to some degree foreseen in the instructing about the entryway (10:9). Reality. Christ as truth makes the way trustworthy and reliable (cf. 1:4; 8:32,36; Eph. 4:20,21). The Life. (cf. 1:4; 11:25). No man cometh. The verb put Jesus in favor of God instead of in favor of man (he doesn't state, "goeth"). "No man accomplish the Father with the exception of by seeing the Truth and taking an interest in the Life which is uncovered to men in His Son.

Along these lines, while being the guide. He doesn't manual for what is past Himself, Knowledge of the Son is the information of God" (Hoskyns, 1940).

7. The wording recommends the followers' inability to know Christ as he truly seemed

to be. In perspective of this last disclosure, notwithstanding, there could be no reason for inability to know the Father and additionally the Son. A few original copies have an alternate perusing - "If ye have come to know me (as ye have), ye should know my Father moreover."

8. Want for target experience is solid - demonstrate to us the Father (cf. Exod. 33:17). Philip felt he knew God, yet not as Father in the close sense Jesus implied when He talked about Him.

9. So long time. It was terribly late for the demand. The Son had been uncovering the Father from the start (10:30). That lay at the base of his central goal (1:18).

10. Without a doubt Philip must trust that there was group of life amongst Father and Son. Out of the union of the Son with the Father came "the words" that Jesus talked. Out of the works which he performed came the showing that the Father was abiding in him and acting through him.

11. The interest moved from Philip to the Eleven. Trust me. That is, acknowledge my declaration about my connection to the Father. An adequately high view Christ makes his

self-revelation the last confirmation. For those that need other confirmation, the works are there to bolster the claim.

12. More prominent works. Not to be limited to the signs, for example, Jesus created in the times of his tissue. The works couldn't be more noteworthy in quality than his, yet more noteworthy in degree. Since I go unto my Father. This is the explanation behind the more prominent works.

The confinements forced on Jesus by incarnation would be evacuated. His position with the Father would be connected in the more prominent works in two ways: noting the petitions of his own, and sending the Paraclete as the unfailing wellspring of knowledge and quality. The works, then, would not be done in freedom of Christ. He would answer petition; he would send the Spirit.

13-14. At all. The extent of petition. Inquire. The state of petition. In my name. The ground of Prayer. This includes no less than two things: supplicating in the expert Christ gives (cf. Matt. 28:19; Acts 3:6) and supplicating in union with him, so one doesn't ask outside His will. That will I do. The sureness of supplication. That the Father might be celebrated in the Son. The reason for petition. In the event that ye should inquire. The "if" is in favor of the person who asks, not in favor of Christ.

15. On the off chance that ye cherish me. This is the climate in which the summon to implore as well as every other order of the Lord will be regarded by his workers. "Keep" is basic in the AV, however great original copy expert requires a future shape - "ye will keep." Love is not essentially a wistful connection; it is the element for acquiescence. My instructions. Eventually, no one but God can order. Divinity was talking.

16. These decrees can be kept just in the force of the Holy Spirit, called here another Comforter. A superior interpretation now would be :assistant." At the time the AV was deciphered, sofa-bed held a greater amount of the first constrain of "strengthener" than it has today. "Another" puts the Spirit in a similar class with Jesus)cf. Phil. 4:13). In the Spirit we have more than an infrequent assistant - that he may live with you for ever.

17. The Spirit of Truth (cf. 15:26; 16:13). He is illuminator and in addition aide. His awesome

topic is Christ the Truth (14:6; 15:26). Whom the world can't get. The world is administered by the faculties. Since the Spirit can't be seen nor fathomed by reason, he stays outside the world's cognizant experience (cf. I Cor. 2:9-14).

Dwelleth with you. A steady nearness, adjusting for the withdrawal of the Lord. In you. Not just with them as a nearness pervading the corporate body, yet abiding in them exclusively.

18. A similar subject is proceeded. Dismal. Vagrants. The need of the devotees would be met when Christ came to them in revival favoring. This would carry with it the happening to the individual of the Spirit (20:22). As clearly as the Spirit would be with them and in them so would Christ.

It is difficult to separate the two, similarly as the Son and the Father are indissoluble (cf. II Cor. 3:17). Christ was not talking here of his future coming, as in verse 3, however of a coming that would meet a prompt need.

19. For just a constrained time would Christ be a question of sight to the world. At that point would come demise, and however it would be trailed by restoration, this would not reestablish him to the eyes of men(Matt. 23:39). It was on

the grounds that these pupils were profoundly alive that they would have the capacity to see him and get to be partakers of his risen life.

20. At that day these men would have the capacity to handle what Jesus had been attempting to educate them concerning his existence with the Father, which was an existence of interpenetration and fellowship, and furthermore about their own particular life, which had now been similarly taken up into the awesome and implanted with it.

Ye should know. Gnoesthe talks about revelation. Obviously, this does not qualifies the devotee for say that he is God or the Son of God. Union is aimless separated from this different presence of the individuals who make it.

21. Jesus came back to the subject of affection and the keeping of his decrees (cf. v. 15), yet in perspective of the educating in verse 20 now included say of the Father. The keeping of Christ's decrees exhibits love for Christ.

This affection welcomes the noting adoration for the Father, whose affection for the Son is to such an extent that he should love all who have love for him. It conveys likewise sign of the Son to the adherent. What the supporters delighted in by method for physical appearance of the risen Lord to themselves taking after the Resurrection, they were to appreciate likewise in an otherworldly sense all through whatever is left of their natural journey.

22. Judas ..... not Iscariot. The notoriety of the deceiver was bad to the point that John takes mind not to allow any perplexity of recognizable proof, regardless of the way that alternate Judas had left the room.

This Judas couldn't comprehend an indication limited to the picked few, not that it was outlandish (that very thing was happening right now) yet that it didn't appear to accord with the wonderfulness of the Messianic office. If Christ somehow happened to return once more, why not to the world? He was confused by Jesus' announcement in verse 19.

23. "The response to Judas is, that the indication alluded to must be restricted, on the grounds that it must be made where there is that fellowship of adoration which substantiates itself by the soul of discipline and accommodation to the charge of Jesus (Milligan and Moulton, 1898).

This sign is extremely individual as well as it prompts to a perpetual connection - make our dwelling place him. Watch that the Son doesn't hesitate to submit the Father to a specific strategy, another reasonable sign of divinity.

24. Here is the conclusion on the negative side of reality of the last verse. Yet again Christ attested the solidarity of the Son's oath with that of the Father.

25-26. These things ..... all things. The instructing of Christ touching the new states of the coming age was suggestive as opposed to finish (cf. 16:12). This insufficiency was to be overcome by the happening to the Holy Spirit. His service to adherents would be, in the fundamental, to show them (one of the immense workplaces of Christ also; the two are consolidated, by suggestion in Acts 1:1).

All things (cf. I Cor. 2:13-15). These matters apparently would in view of the individual and work of Christ, accordingly managing a continuation of Jesus' instructing. A part of the Spirit's work, indeed, would be that of reviewing what Christ had talked (cf. 2:22; 12:16).

27. Peace. A continuous word regarding goodbyes (cf. Eph. 6:23; I Peter 5:14). Be that as it may, this is a legacy instead of just a routine touch. Leave (aphiemi) is infrequently utilized as

a part of this sense. Another case happens in the LXX of Ps. 17:14. My tranquility. A particular brand of peace, unique in relation to that of the world, which would be hysterical at such a hour as this, with death so close. The endowment of his tranquility would make his adherents unafraid, as he seemed to be (cf. 16:33).

28. The Lord had no expectation of concealing the reality of his flight, yet he helped them that the bitterness to remember takeoff was diminished by his guarantee to return once more. In the event that ye cherished me.

Their affection was yet inadequate. Adore wishes the best for the person who is cherished. The pupils ought to have celebrated in his arrival to the Father.

My Father is more prominent than I. This has nothing to do with fundamental being, and does not negate John 10:30 and different sections. The Father was in position to compensate the Son for dutifulness unto passing. There is an insight here that endowments would originate from Christ's arrival to the Father that would profit his adherents; so their delight would not be altogether impartial.

29. All the overflowed gift without bounds

would support the expression of Christ and would build the certainty and confidence of the pupils in him.

30. The Prince of this world (cf. 12:31). A reference to Satan. Here the prompt criticalness is by all accounts the treachery by Judas, the instrument of Satan, and the capture of Jesus (cf. Luke 22:53). Hath nothing in me. No partake in Christ's individual or cause (cf. 13:8). There might be a recommendation here of reality that Satan has nothing in Christ which is legitimately his own, which he can claim or lay hold of for his own advantage. Christ is pure and triumphant over fiendishness.

31. The very thing that Satan was going to impact, in particular, the demise of Christ on the cross, was the thing which the Savior was squeezing forward to do. In any case, he did it not as the vulnerable casualty of Satan but rather out of adoration for the Father, knowing it was the Father's rule (his communicated will).

Emerge, let us go consequently. It is in no way, shape or form sure that the charge was done promptly. There is trouble in assuming that whatever is left of the talk could have been talked in an open place, even in the Temple.

CHAPTER

FIFTEEN

Strands of Thought Discernible (15:1-27)

In Chapter 15 the accompanying strands of believed are perceptible: natural product bearing through dwelling in Christ (vv. 1-11); cherish as the preeminent organic product (vv. 12-17); the contempt of the world for the pupil, with respect to Christ (vv. 18-25); the awesome and human observer to Christ (vv. 25-27).

1. I am the genuine vine. A balance is presumably proposed with Israel, a vine of God's planting which demonstrated unfruitful (Isa. 5:1-7). Genuine. Genuine, all that a vine ought to be in a profound sense. Christ is not simply the root or stock, but rather the entire plant. Incorporated into him are his kin. Farmer. Both proprietor and overseer.

2. Each branch in me. To be in Christ is an otherworldly actuality of endless significance. Beareth not organic product. This is no future devotee. As there are suckers that become out from the plant however add nothing to its convenience and must be removed, so an ineffective offspring of God who endures in his own will may hope to be put aside.

God's reprimanding hand may even evacuate such a man through death. He purgeth it. This applies to the productive branch. It is kept clean of any propensity to deadness or to negligible development of the branch as unmistakable from creation of organic product. The protest is more natural product.

3. Clean through (truly, as a result of) the word. Set apart from others by having gotten God's disclosure in Christ.

4. Dwell in me, and I in you. This reviews 14:20. Be that as it may, there the idea identifies with position; here it identifies with volition, the choice to depend deliberately upon Christ as the state of productivity. Christ's answer is an internal sign - I in you. A branch separated from the vine is essentially unfruitful. An indispensable union is in view.

5. The vine and the branches are recognized. From the vine comes the life; from the branches, accordingly, comes the organic product. The request is the same here as in 14:20 and 15:4. Our living in Christ associates us with the wellspring of life. His living in us brings an enduring supply of organic product - much

natural product. Without me. Aside from me, separated from me.

6. Apart from delivering grapes the vine has no utilization but to be singed for fuel (cf. Ezek. 15:6). Men .... they. "The uncertainty of the subject compares with the secrecy of the demonstration symbolized" (Westcott, 1896). Since the subject is the direction of foods grown from the ground everlasting life, the blazing is a judgment upon pointlessness, not a surrender to endless devastation.

The branch is the capability of conceivable organic product bearing, not the individual himself. It talks here of unfruitful works (cf. I Cor. 3:15).

7. The expressions of Christ, and also the individual of Christ, may live in the adherent. It is the instructing of Christ that offers ascend to the best possible sort of imploring. At the point when the expression of Christ stays lavishly inside (Col. 3:16), one may securely ask what he will, and it should be finished. The instructing is like that in John 14:13, 14.

8. Discipleship is a developing, dynamic thing. The more natural product we bear, the all the more really are we satisfying the example

of pupils, the individuals who learn of Christ with a specific end goal to resemble him. God is celebrated in this way. He is vindicated and remunerated for his interest in the vineyard.

9. The say of adoration in this association proposes this is the central thing in the natural product which the Father is worried to discover in his kids (cf. Lady. 5:22). Be that as it may, this is not love in a general sense - rather, my adoration, the affection for Christ. When he comes into stand, he carries his adoration with him, which thusly is the very love delighted in by Christ from the Father.

Christian love turns out to be in this manner divine in character. Proceed ye in my affection. Acknowledge no substitutes.

10. The delight in the Savior's adoration is molded on keeping his charges. This is no subjective prerequisite, for Christ has worked under this lead himself in his connection to the Father. The pupil is not over his Lord.

11. The life of affection produces bliss. Christ had it to start with, as the aftereffect of doing flawlessly the Father's will and making the most of his adoration. This is granted to his own, and in the process gets to be distinctly

customized in order to wind up distinctly their bliss. Ownership might be fractional at to begin with, yet the objective is to be full, ruling out dread or disappointment.

12-13. The following area starts and finishes with the summon to love each other. Here is an encapsulating of the Christian's commitment. It is no longer an advice to keep Christ's charges so as to stay in his adoration (v. 10). It is fairly a directive to focus on the one rule to have love for each other. As I have cherished (loved) you.

The measure of Christ's adoration for his own particular is his altruism in which they advantage (cf. I John 3:16). Such a standard can be met just at Christ's own particular love is allowed to course through the term of his kin. The Synoptic declarations of the cross by Jesus underscore its celestial need; here the inspiration is love.

The cross is not something forced but rather something grasped - set out his life. Quick confirmation of adoration is the readiness to give propel sign of the reason to bite the dust for the individuals who are companions. Demise for them in no astute negates the reason to bite the dust for a bigger circle, even the world itself.

14. Fellowship with Jesus does not wipe out the need for compliance.

15. In the event that this need appears to make hirelings out of companions, there is a distinction. The worker is not taken into the certainty of his master. Evidence of the status of companions, on account of the devotees, was their admission to the guidance of Christ, including all that the Father had uncovered to the Son. Nothing had been withheld. This does not imply that all had been comprehended by Jesus' supporters.

16. Keeping in mind that the devotees get the feeling that only they were in the arrangements of God, Christ clarified that they had been allowed their favored position with a view to their proclaiming the message to others. They had been picked, not with a view to their own particular joy or pride.

Or maybe, Christ appointed (selected) them on account of administration. Go.... deliver organic product. Beforehand the natural product implied love. Presently it was to mean love in real life, the proclaiming of the message of salvation and the triumphant of souls. There is a nearby association in thought with John 12:24.

Remain. A similar word has been interpreted "withstand" prior in the part. That there would tolerate organic product was a thoughtful guarantee in perspective of the disillusioning outcomes amid Jesus' own service, with many purporting an enthusiasm for him, just to abandon him after a period.

17. This verse is transitional. The followers needed to share love among themselves, for they would not get it from the world. Now "adore" everything except vanishes from the section, being supplanted by "detest" or "contempt" (eight circumstances in the same number of verses).

18. The world. Unredeemed society, alienated from God, held in the hold of wrongdoing and the detestable one, heedless to profound truth and threatening to the individuals who have the life of God in them. Contempt would not be gone to upon the devotees in a soul of against Semitism, yet as a continuation of the antagonistic vibe and disdain went to upon Christ. The assault would move from the Shepherd to the sheep. As unquestionably as their lives would reflect Christ, so doubtlessly would they draw in the contempt of corrupt men (cf. Lady. 4:29).

19. Threatening vibe is established in otherworldly difference. The world is agreeable within the sight of its own. It is fit for a specific warmth for such. The selectiveness of the Christian culture, a recovered group inside an unredeemed, energizes dismay. Reprimanded by the sacredness of the individuals who are Christ's (cf. v.22), the world demonstrates its hatred.

20. The evidence of validity in discipleship is the correspondence between the response of men to the service of Jesus' adherents and the response of men to Christ in the times of his tissue. A few men would oppress them; others would keep their assertion. Keep in mind the word.

The reference is to John 13:16. Acts 4:13 is an effective outline of Jesus' instructing here. Having freed themselves of Jesus, as they thought, the rulers were daunted to get themselves confronted by pupils who went about as he did.

21. For my name's purpose. Christ endured dismissal since men did not by any stretch of the imagination know the One who sent him. The devotees were being accepted into the hover of the misjudged, imparting this qualification to their Lord.

22. This numbness of Christ's character and mission was grounded in the wrongdoing of men. Despite the fact that Christ had not come to judge yet rather to spare, yet his extremely nearness and witness blended up indications of wrongdoing that generally would have stayed lethargic.

Uncovered by the Savior, his foes had no concealing spot. Their one resort was to expel Christ from before their eyes. They had not had sin. The finishing sin of unbelief and dismissal the Savior.

23. The cost of detesting Christ is the judgment of despising the Father also. Men can't treat the Father in one way and the Son in another.

24. The "works" (supplementing the expression of Christ in v. 22) were of such a character, to the point that men needed to go to a decision for or against him. In dismissing him, they had sin. It was sin joined by scorn which consistently included the Father in whose name the Son had come.

25. Their law. The very Scriptures which the Jews gloried in rose up to censure them (Ps. 69:4). Without a cause (dorean). Such contempt is shaky. It does not have all ground in the person

who is detested. A similar word happens, with a similar significance, in Romans 3:24, where the ground of salvation is displayed as being God himself and not the value of man. Such disdain requests a solid and dauntless declaration to the world. John now depicts the way of this witness.

26-27. The followers would not confront the world alone. They would have a heavenly partner, the Spirit of Truth. He would squeeze home reality about men's wicked condition and reality (truth) about Christ, the remedy for that sin.

The Spirit was to go under a twofold commission, in a manner of speaking, being sent of the Son from the Father, keeping in mind the end goal to affirm of Christ (cf. 16:7-13). Ye additionally give testimony. Most likely characteristic as opposed to basic. From the point of view of relationship with Jesus, which had given them the information important for a legitimate witness, they were qualified now, since they had been with him from the earliest starting point - from the beginning of the service. However, to be compelling, their witness must be joined to that of the Spirit working in them and through them (cf. Acts 5:32).

CHAPTER

SIXTEEN

The Departure Of Christ
And
The Anticipation Of What
This World Would Mean
(16:1-33)

The Spirit was to go under a twofold commission, as it were, being sent of the Son from the Father, keeping in mind the end goal to affirm of Christ (cf. 16:7-13). Ye additionally take the stand. Most likely characteristic as opposed to basic. From the outlook of relationship with Jesus, which had given them the learning vital for a legitimate witness, they were qualified now, since they had been with him from the earliest starting point - from the beginning of the service. However, to be compelling, their witness must be joined to that of the Spirit working in them and through them (cf. Acts 5:32).

In Chapter 16 the prevailing note continues as before - the takeoff of Christ and the suspicion of what this world mean. The idea moves along the accompanying lines: Christ's notice of coming abuse (10:1-4a); his flight clarified in the light of the happening to the Spirit and his service to adherents (16:12-15); solaces to counterbalance the torment of partition (16:16-28); the triumph of the Son of God (16:29-33).

The subject of abuse had been foreseen by the past educating (ch. 15) on the contempt of the world for Christ and his own.

1. These things have I talked unto you. Essentially the data about the scorn of the world, so that the followers may be forearmed, additionally the update that they were observers to that exceptionally world which would disdain them (cf. 15:27). Duty hardens character. That ye ought not be outraged. "Offended" presents bumbling in light of a hindrance in the way instead of due to an inward inclination to deserting.

On this record the RSV rendering, to shield you from falling ceaselessly, is not entirely tasteful. Jesus' typical expression is, "outraged in me" (Luke 7:23; Matt. 26:31).

2. Out of the synagogues (cf. 9:22). A most difficult ordeal to a Jew, whose tie with the country was solid. Jewish professors in Jerusalem kept on blending with their kinsmen in the Temple after Pentecost, demonstrating their feeling of family relationship with their kin.

Will surmise that he doeth God benefit. The best concerning his mistreating days (Acts 26:9-11). He quantified his energy for his own religion by the dread and assaults he perpetrated on the congregation (Gal. 1:13; Phil 3:6).

3. Numbness of Christ and his actual connection to the Father represents mistreatment. Such obliviousness does not make the persecutor passable. Paul marked himself head of heathens on this very record! (I Tim. 1:13-15).

4. At the point when abuse would strike, the memory of Christ's reliability in notice of these things would serve to fortify his workers. To meet such things ill-equipped would bring alarm. I was with you. Christ was their shield against resistance. In the light of his soon leaving, the present educating went up against a hugeness it couldn't have had some time recently.

It was currently to contemplate this flight and about what it would mean for the individuals who remained.

5. For Christ the going implied an arrival to the One who had sent him. This part of it had not laid hold of the psyches of the supporters to state any degree. They had not asked, Whither goest thou?

6. Rather, they had been engrossed with their feeling of misfortune. They were in the hold of distress.

7. It is practical for you that I leave. The disservice regarding detachment and distress was to be exceeded by the pick up occasioned by the happening to the Comforter (aide). One has just to think about the followers toward the finish of Jesus' service with these same men after the happening to the Spirit to perceive how incredibly they had progressed in comprehension and in the adequacy of their administration.

In the event that I go not ..... the Comforter (Holy Spirit) won't come (cf. 7:37-39). This is not an indication of threatening vibe or envy between the Son and the Spirit. In fact, the Spirit had happened upon Christ to engage him for his work,; and soon he would happen upon Christ's supporters, as if to make up for the loss of the individual nearness of the Lord.

8. He will decry the world. Upbraid may similarly well be rendered "convict" or "persuade." The Spirit was to start things out to the devotees (see end of v. 7), and through them he would attempt his central goal of sentencing men.

One might say this service associates with the world's movement of oppression.

The world may seem to make advances on the Church, yet there is a counterattack in the work of the Spirit, outlined not to hurt but rather to change over, or if nothing else to convict. The Spirit, working through the witnesses, created conviction of wrongdoing in the very city where Jesus had been executed (Acts 2:37).

9. Of transgression. For the reason that the transgression of the world came to sharp concentration in the dismissal of Jesus when there ought to have been acknowledgment of him, the Spirit makes this the essential issue. In their visual deficiency men were calling Jesus a heathen at the very time their own particular sin was driving them to execute him.

10. Of uprightness. The very reality that Christ could tackle the transgression issue of humankind by his recovering passing uncovered his ideal honesty.

Else he would have required a Savior for himself. The Father is the genuine judge of honorableness. His preparation to get the Son once more into radiance is the evidence that he found in him no insufficiency (Rom. 1:4; 4:25; I Tim.3:16).

11. Of Judgment. At the point when the individuals who killed Jesus saw that God did not meddle, they envisioned that the judgment of God was being articulated on him. Really, another was being judged there, even Satan, the sovereign of this world. Satan controls by method for transgression and passing.

Christ's triumph over transgression at the traverse demise at the Resurrection proclaimed the way that Satan had been judged. The execution of conclusive judgment is just a short time.

Now the idea moves far from the world. The Spirit's work for the benefit of devotees comes into view.

12. The talk was not an entire work of the musings of Jesus toward his own. Held for possible later use were numerous things. It was futile to wander upon them, for the devotees couldn't bear them. They were excessively juvenile. These truths would turn out to be all the more genuine to them as their experience developed.

13. The correspondence of these things could be securely conceded until the Spirit of truth came, who is the instructor as genuinely as the Lord himself. All truth.

Not truth in each domain of learning, but rather truth in the things of God in the smaller sense, which we discuss as otherworldly things (cf. I Cor. 2:10).

He might not discuss (from) himself. He would not endeavor to start the things he would educate, yet like the Son (15:15), would pass on to men what was given to him from God the Father. On basic source ensures solidarity in the educating. At last devotees are instructed of God (I Thess. 4:9). Things to come. The arrival of Christ and orderly occasions might be in view, however more quickly the "things to come" were the demise and revival of Jesus and their belongings, the very things over which the supporters had faltered when Jesus has discussed them.

14. Extol. Eve as Christ was commending the Father by his compliance unto passing, so the Spirit would extol Christ by clarifying the hugeness of his individual and work. The Spirit's showing mission would be first to "get" the store of Christ-focused truth, then show it to adherents.

It takes after that a service, to be Spirit-coordinated, must be one that amplifies Christ.

15. Since the things of Christ incorporate the truths concerning the Father and his advice, when the Spirit conveys the things of Christ, he imparts every bit of relevant information.

Next the Lord managed the remunerations that ought to facilitate the agony occasioned by his flight. These incorporated the guarantee that the devotees would see him once more (v. 16); their bliss at seeing him (v. 22); the benefit of supplication (vv. 23,24); expanded learning (v. 25); and the supporting affection for the Father for them (v. 27).

16. A short time. The expression happens seven circumstances in four verses. This alludes to the short interim that stayed before his entombment, when the pupils would no longer observe him with the eyes of physical sight. The second "short time" assigns the interim between his entombment and his revival, after which they would see him once more.

Here "see" is not the same as in the primary event. It passes on here the prospect of discernment and also of perception. Something of the importance of this show of reclamation, which was currently so puzzling, would first light upon these men. The last condition, "since

I go to the Father," does not have adequate composition specialist to be held in the content.

17. The expressions of Jesus were outside the ability to comprehend of the pupils. People among them had made inquiries before this. These men (some of his supporters), excessively bashful, making it impossible to voice their perplexity straightforwardly met with on another as opposed to tending to the Lord.

In this verse the words, "since I go to the Father," are bona fide. They are effortlessly clarified on the premise of Jesus utilization of them in verse 10. The reality of his flight is the all-retaining concern.

19-20. Perceiving their passionate longing to have a response to the issue of the "short time" in its twofold application, Jesus offered to supply an answer, yet not the exact answer they were seeking after. However, he indicated what the "short time" would mean for them in each example.

In the previous, they would sob while the world cheered, for the demise of the Savior would bring absolutely extraordinary responses from adherents than from the general population of the world (cf. Rev. 11:10). In any case, the very thing that would bring distress would be transformed into an event of "happiness" when the followers could see the cross in the light of the Resurrection, when the second "short time" would break upon them.

21. Jesus drew a similarity from human life for the supplanting of distress with satisfaction. A lady's travail torments bring distress, yet she overlooks her agony in the delight of the birth. It might be noteworthy that a man is said to be conceived (instead of a youngster).

Christ in restoration as the main conceived from the dead (Col. 1:18) joins with himself the new man, "His Church," to which he bestows his risen life.

22. The delight of get-together would be a standing knowledge; the second partition, occasioned by the Lord's rising, would not influence that bliss (Luke 24:51-53).

23. In that day. The Lord was thinking about the conditions that would win after his arrival to the Father. In the middle of the road time of the forty days after the Resurrection, the supporters asked something (Acts 1:6). Be that as it may, when he was taken up, all open door for inquiries, for example, were currently being

asked would be gone. This does not mean there would be add up to absence of correspondence. The entryway of supplication would be open.

On the off chance that they would however "ask," the Father would "give" the solutions to their perplexities and would address their issues. In my name (see the remark 14:13,14).

24. Asked nothing. Here "solicited" is utilized as a part of the sense from making a request of instead of encircling a question. Because of the nearness of Jesus in their middle, asking in his name had been pointless. Yet, in the new day that was coming, their "satisfaction" at seeing Jesus again would be kept up by this intercourse of supplication.

25. Precepts. No adages, yet cloud expressions. His lessons were regularly enigmatical (a question) to his supporters. Yet, a change was coming. "The arrival of Jesus to the Father introduced another time, in which the Lord addresses His teaches no longer unclearly however plainly and straightforwardly; it is assumed that the perusers of the Gospel comprehend that He addresses them through the Spirit which they have gotten" (Hoskyns, 1940).

26-27. Later on, petition would without a doubt be for the sake of Christ, however not as in the Son would be the method for conquering some kind of reluctance or resistance in the Father which generally adherents would experience.

In actuality, the Father "loveth" them, and is prepared to get them as a result of their state of mind toward his cherished Son. As opposed to the world, they have cherished and believed the Son as the one sent by God.

28. What the confidence of the devotees ought to incorporate is currently put forward in its easiest and boldest blueprint. The main portion of the announcement had been avowed more than once by at least one of the gathering; the second part manages the weight of this talk, the leaving of their pioneer. Presently he put this takeoff forcefully and unmistakably - I leave the world, and go to the Father.

Now the talk was practically closed. It finished on a twofold note - the woeful disappointment of those Jesus had attempted to train, and his own triumph, helped by the nearness of the Father.

29-30. Energized alike by the tribute of

their confidence and by the plain talking about Jesus concerning his profession the supporters envisioned that they were lolling in the prevalent learning of the Son of God.

31-32. A severe shock was in store for them. They would be "scattered" (at the season of the capture of Jesus) and he would be allowed to sit unbothered, yet he would have the assistance of the Father.

33. For their insurance he gave his tranquility (cf. 14:27), which they would require as they confronted the tribulation in store for them on the planet. This is peace in the midst of contention, as well as peace which rests in the affirmation of a triumph now won by their champion over the world. Christ's triumph is the target reality which makes substantial the internal endowment of his tranquility.

CHAPTER

SEVENTEEN

The Great Prayer
(17:1-26)

At the end of the goodbye address of Moses, we have recorded in Deuteronomy 32 an incredible supplication which is known as the Song of Moses. As per John's Gospel, our Lord finishes up his last talk with his pupils with a supplication that could likewise be called "The Great Prayer" or "A Song" or "Psalm." It is the satisfaction of the Song of Moses. The vindication of Yahweh in the petition of Jesus is discussed as now total. The hour of that vindication is here.

This supplication draws together a considerable lot of the topics that are available in the last talk instructing and furthermore subjects that we find in the petition Jesus showed his supporters are recorded in alternate Gospels. That concise petition, the "Our Father" (Matt. 6:7-13), opens with the acknowledgment of the magnificence and rule of God. This petition of Jesus in John 17 likewise starts with the acknowledgment of God's brilliance now uncovered in the Son.

The "Our Father" petition appeals to God

for the royal rule of God upon the earth. This petition requests sacred quality for the followers to experience the rule of God on the earth. The "Our Father" requests pardoning; here Jesus claims for his teaches the wholeness that come in absolution: "Purify them in reality."

The "Our Father" request quality to pardon others; in this supplication Jesus asks that his affection might be in them. The "Our Father" request assurance against the abhorrent one; in this petition similar words show up: "that thou shouldest keep them from the underhanded one."

Jesus starts this supplication, "Father, the hour has come; laud thy Son." The emotional expression "the hour" or "my hour" has been utilized all through John's Gospel unequivocally. By this expression we find that God's powerful will is satisfied in a specific occasion, a minute, 60 minutes. God's affection, in this way, is not a general truth or foremost but rather the adoration that thinks solidly about genuine individuals in genuine spots.

God's forceful will is God's relentless demonstration, and that demonstration occurred ever. This solidness does not reduce the immortal unceasing importance of that hour. All of paradise and earth from the earliest starting point to the finish of time looks to that hour in amazement.

From this "Extraordinary Prayer" we find that Christ is celebrated in the restoration as well as by his mortification at Calvary. It is in Jesus who passes on and is triumphant over death that we see the nearness of God getting through to us. The transcendence of God is more than the show of enormity and superbness. It is the show of embarrassment and lowliness. It is the Jesus with the towel and bowl of water and also the Jesus who overcomes the visual deficiency of the young fellow on the sanctuary steps.

Along these lines, Jesus petition asks that God the Father will show himself, his character, in the entire arrangement of occasions that now will happen. We are so adapted to consider grandness in triumphal terms that we regularly overlook what's really important of the supplication. This is a petition on the eve of the aggregate servanthood of Jesus Christ.

In that astonishing beauty of Jesus Christ, the worker Lord, we will see the wonderfulness of God! That he is so solid to have the capacity to achieve so far down! How beyond any doubt of himself to take even upon himself our passing.

Jesus included himself in this petition (vv. 1-5), yet his central concern was for his own. In both areas the component of commitment is emphatically blended with appeal.

1. Father. Utilized routinely in Jesus' supplications, six circumstances here. The hour is come. The time is unclear, as something surely understood amongst Father and Son. It was without a moment's delay the ideal opportunity for affliction and for glorification.

Praise thy Son. Empower him to satisfy his course, fulfilling the salvation for which he came. Evidently Christ did not look for some respect here for his own purpose, for in his own particular glorification through death, restoration, and magnification, he looked for just to celebrate the Father.

2. This glorification of the Father incorporates into it the height of the Son to eminence and power, where he is head over all things (cf. Matt. 28:18). "Control" implies expert. Here it has particularly in view the allowing of "interminable life," on the premise of Christ's done work.

The recipients are portrayed as those whom the Father has given to the Son. This is a portrayal of the pupils which repeats frequently all through the supplication (vv. 2,6,9,11,12,24).

3. Everlasting life is put forward as far as knowing God (cf. I John 5:20). The Jews did not know God, however they knew much about him. It is the claim of this verse and this entire Gospel that the learning of God which brings endless life comes just through the information of the Son.

Since the Father and the Son are one, the information is one. The learning of God suggests the information of his courses and also of his individual, thus incorporates the impression of his arrangement of salvation from wrongdoing. Jesus Christ (cf. 1:17). Uncommon in the Gospels however basic in the Epistles.

4. I have celebrated thee on the earth. This is our Lord clarified as far as completing the work the Father offered him to do - the disclosure of the Father, the presentation of transgression, the decision and preparing of the Twelve, and above all the demise on the cross, which was certain to the point that it could be viewed as effectively finished. "Completed" means culminated and finished.

5. Having talked about his work on the earth (v.4), the Son now looked for glorification with the Father in the magnificent domain. So the differentiation is twofold, comprising of place and individual. With thine claim self …. with thee. In thy nearness. Prior to the world was. (cf. 1:1,2).

Verses 6-8 are transitional, as yet managing the work of Christ on earth yet paving the way to the petitions for the pupils.

6. A huge part of the work of the Son on the earth had been to make the Father known to the devotees (cf. 1:14; 14:7-9). The accomplishment of this procedure is suggested in the way that these men were God's blessing to the Son. Their comprehension was not flawless, but rather it was certain and developing.

They have kept my assertion. Not a reference basically to their dutifulness to individual summons or lessons, yet to their status to get the Son, his message and mission, in so far as they were capable.

7-8. The supporters had progressed to the point of understanding that the character and endowments and works of Christ must be followed to the imperceptible God, in whose name he had come. Specifically the supporters had laid hold of the disclosure of truth in Christ, remembering it as really of God.

They had in this way achieved a state of improvement where it was protected to abandon them. In their future work they would speak to one who himself had spoken to the living God. Thou didst send me. This expression resonates through the petition (vv. 3,8,18,21,23,25). It was a continuous claim of Christ in his talks.

Having named the capabilities of the pupils as his agents on the planet, the Lord now intervened for them.

9. I ask not for the world. This does not imply that Christ never appealed to God for the world (cf. Luke 23:34). Be that as it may, he petitioned God for the pupils since they were the picked medium of achieving the world after he himself had abandoned it (vv. 21,23).

10. All mine are thine. In this manner the worry of the Son to petition God for these men and the worry of the Father to hear and answer are indistinguishable justifiable. The exclusive intrigue is common. I am celebrated in them. The precursor of "them" might be the things held in like manner by Father and Son, or better,

the followers who have been specified in the past verse.

It was to the magnificence of Christ that in the midst of general unbelief and dismissal, these men set out to trust and serve him. "Glorified" is in the ideal tense, proposing the continuation of their declaration to Christ.

The main particular request of was for the protection of the followers from the malicious that is on the planet (vv. 11-15). This thusly was to fill another need, one which is vigorously underscored in whatever is left of the petition, specifically, that they may be one.

11. Keep. Utilized as a part of the feeling of defensive oversight, as in I John 5:18. The character of God as totally different from malice and along these lines intrigued by saving his youngsters, is underlined in the address, Holy Father. On the positive side, this protection would make the devotees one, mirroring the unity amongst Father and Son. The bond is the sacred love of God. This solidarity is found in the early church (Acts 1:14; 2:1,44,46).

12. The best validated Greek content understands, I was keeping them in thy name which thou gavest to me. Not exclusively did

Jesus keep his own particular trains by the expert of the Father, however he kept them by reality and force of the way of God, which he himself uncovered.

The Son of condemnation. "Perdition" is from an indistinguishable root from "lost." Jesus was stating that the misfortune was not a reflection on His keeping influence as the shepherd of the rush. Or maybe, Judas had never truly had a place with him aside from in an ostensible, outer sense (cf. 13:10,11). The thought in condemnation is precisely the inverse of protection. The sacred text. (Ps. 41:9).

13. What's more, now come I to thee. Thus lay the event for entire petition and every one of the solicitations contained in it. The devotees' requirement for "bliss" was especially intense in light of Judas' surrender. The pupils expected to understand that such a case did not think about the Lord or on themselves.

It was not to deface their happiness in the ownership of genuine confidence and life. On the off chance that Christ could cheer even amidst such things (my satisfaction), they ought to do as such moreover.

14. The gathering of the expression of Christ

recognized these men with him and set them apart from the world, which dismisses and despised him and in this way had a similar disposition toward them.

15. Regardless of the solidarity amongst Christ and his own, he couldn't implore that the Father would remove them from the world. To do as such would have disappointed the motivation behind their call and preparing. As they worked and saw, they should have been kept from the fiendishness; generally their witness would have stopped to be unadulterated. The reference may well be to the detestable one himself (cf. Matt. 6:13; I Peter 5:8).

16. As recovered men, the pupils no longer had a place with the world as a domain of profound malevolent, despite the fact that they lived on the planet as a physical element.

17. Purify them through thy truth. This is the second appeal to for the benefit of the devotees. "Purify" intends to separate for God and sacred purposes. That which uncovers the blessed will of God in his truth, and particularly that truth as cherished in the expression of Scripture. There one realizes what God requires and how he empowers one to satisfy the prerequisite.

18. To be sent into the world by Christ as he was sent by the Father is the most noteworthy nobility that can be presented on men.

19. Christ did not have to make himself blessed, for he was that. In any case, he needed to give (bless) himself to his calling, that he teaches may have not his case but rather message to announce, and the power got from his relinquish whereby to broadcast it adequately.

20-21. The supplication contacts incorporate the individuals who will trust on account of the declaration of these men (cf. 10:16; Acts 18:10). Confidence is the fundamental condition for getting a charge out of the life of God and hence of coming into that solidarity which is discovered as a matter of first importance in the Godhead and after that in the group of Christ, the Church. The solidarity is essentially individual - in us. Its impact will be to evoke confidence with respect to those on the planet (cf. 13:35).

22. The wonderfulness. Certainly this focuses to a definitive brilliant position of the Church, however it incorporates the benefit of serving and sufferings, similarly as the Father gave this commission on the Son. This benefit

binds together the holy people as it is practiced in the light of Christ our trailblazer inside the cover.

23. Made flawless in one. To be proficient not by human exertion, but rather by the generous expansion of the solidarity of the Godhead to the individuals who have a place with Christ. This is not a mechanical solidarity. Its bond is the adoration for God offered on men, that same love (sublime to relate) which the Father has for the Son.

24. The last appeal. I Will. The Spirit of the Incarnation was, Not my will however thine be finished. It must be that Jesus was asking in the light of his completed work, which qualified him for communicate in this form.

His will, certainly, is not to be considered as something truly autonomous of the will of God. This appeal to expands on the last. To take an interest in the affection for God in Christ can just outcome in the end in sharing the nearness of Christ - with me where I am. Union prompts to fellowship, a fellowship of adoration showed in a setting of wonderfulness (cf. v5).

25. Exemplary Father. He is honest (1) in barring the world from that radiance, since it

has not known him and along these lines does not love him, thus can have no place in that last solidarity, and (2) in including the individuals who have come to know him through the information that Christ grants.

26. Giving the learning of God means conferring love, for God is love. This is not only a name or an icy property. Christ knew the truth and force of the affection for the Father for him and asked this may light up and warm the lives of the individuals who were his, with whom his life was presently so firmly bound up.

CHAPTER

EIGHTEEN

The Sufferings And The Glory:
The Betrayal
(18:1-14)

John's record stresses the balance of Jesus and his preparation to be taken, making unnecessary the foul play of Judas from one perspective and the endeavored show of steadfastness by Peter on the other. Included here is the record of the capture and the exchange of Jesus to the esteemed cleric's home.

1. Taking after the supplication, Jesus drove his pupils over the creek Kidron. "Brook" signifies a stream that streams in the winter. A garden on the eastern side was the goal. Matthew and Mark give the name as Gethsemane. John says nothing in regards to the anguish in the garden, however he indicates consciousness of the supplication battle that occurred there (cf. v.11).

We don't know why he overlooked this occurrence. Maybe he was trying to offer unmistakable quality to the component of trust in the state of mind of Jesus, which had as of now been communicated in petition (17:4) and was currently found in his bearing and activity.

2. Ofttimes (cf. Luke 22:39). It might have been the standard thing for Jesus and his organization to spend the night there (Luke 21:37). Judas consequently knew where to search for the Lord on this night.

3. Judas, as well, had a taking after when he entered the garden, however what a differentiating cluster! The band of fighters (Gr. speira) signifies a Roman associate, regularly six hundred men, yet not really at full quality on this event. They were quartered in the Castle of Antonia, at the northern edge of the sanctuary zone (cf. Acts 21:31ff.).

Evidently the Jewish experts could call upon these powers for help in any crisis that debilitated general society intrigue. The city was loaded with travelers going to the devour, a hefty portion of whom were thoughtful to Jesus and might have given inconvenience on the off chance that they had been adjacent when he was being caught.

Officers. These were the sanctuary police who were in the administration of the Jewish rulers (cf. Acts 5:22). They bore lights for looking out their quarry and conveyed weapons for putting down any resistance that may be advertised.

4. Knowing all things. This is a firmly checked element of the Johnannine introduction of the Christ, and has uncommon unmistakable quality in connection to the occasions of the Passion (cf. 13:1,3). Nothing overwhelmed our Lord. Went forward. Cf. 18:1 and the oft-rehashed accentuation upon the more epochal going forward of the Son from the Father into the world, e.g., 16:28.

Whom look for ye? The question served to put the approaching host immediately on edge and committed them to express that their single target was Jesus. This made it simpler for him to ask that the supporters be allowed to go their direction.

5. By replying, Jesus of Nazareth, the group demonstrated that they didn't remember him, because of the semidarkness and their separation from him. I am he. Actually, I am. This statement can show only distinguishing proof, as in 9:9, or it can propose the puzzling and great name of God himself (8:58). Maybe both components are melded for this situation. Judas.... remained with them. Finally he was in his own component, blending with the adversaries of Jesus.

6. Nothing phenomenal is inferred here. The heading of Jesus, in addition to the way that he progressed toward them instead of looked for flight, frightened his captors. Keep in mind that some of these same men had gotten themselves not able to lay hands on him beforehand (7:45,46). Doubtlessly the greatness of his last expression had something to do with their response too.

7-9. At the point when the group admitted again that their goal was Jesus of Nazareth, he could the all the more promptly ask that the devotees be allowed to take off. Their physical security on this event might be viewed as a token that their profound conservation was guaranteed (cf. 6:39; 17:12).

10-11. Dwindle's activity in falling back on utilization of the sword is reasonable in perspective of his presentation of faithfulness in John 13:37. His ownership of a sword is clarified by Christ's guidance in Luke 22:35-38. The sword was typical of days of stress lying ahead, yet was not planned for strict utilize.

Subsequently Jesus' reproach. John's specify of the name of the worker and his ear is an observer touch. Malchus was not one of the officers but rather an individual slave of the devout cleric.

121-14. The Arrest. With Jesus himself calling for non-resistance, the band of troopers, drove by their chief and helped by the Jewish officers, took (caught) Jesus and bound him. They would not like to hazard any slip in their arrangements.

The Synoptists tell about Jesus appearance before Caiaphas, yet say nothing in regards to Annas in this association. Initially calls consideration of the peruser to material now being provided supplementary to the Synoptic records.

In spite of the fact that Annas' child in-law, Caiaphas, was the genuine esteemed cleric as of now, Annas himself was a long way from inert. Notwithstanding Caiaphas, Annas had a few children who succeeded him in this office, giving this one family a restraining infrastructure on the high brotherhood for over a large portion of a century. Luke is the main other essayist who notices Annas (Luke 3:2; Acts 4:6).

Jewish sources name the administration of Annas as degenerate. The direction of Caiaphas about Jesus had as of now been conveyed to the Sanhedrin (11:49,50).

Jesus On Trial
(18:15-27)

15. Prodded by his announcement of reliability to the Master within the sight of the supporters, Peter took after Jesus. Another pupil. This figure, anonymous, might be thought to be John himself. Known unto the consecrated cleric. The word known is discovered again in Luke 2:44; 23:49.

This association, to be followed, likely, through his mom and her family, empowered John to secure affirmation for Peter to the internal court. Royal residence. Yard.

17. The young lady who went about as doorkeeper, most likely expecting Peter's association with Jesus since she knew about John's, tested him to announce himself, and got a refusal.

18. Directly Peter wound up with the captors of Jesus, warming himself by a fire in the yard. John interferes with the account of Peter's disavowal keeping in mind the end goal to provide details regarding the procedures inside, where Jesus was being inspected.

19-20. The high priest.... asked Jesus. Annas

is clearly implied. This was not a trial, for the Sanhedrin had not been gathered; rather it was a hearing to motivate proof to submit to that body when it was assembled a couple of hours after the fact.

The request touched Jesus' devotees and teaching. It is uncertain that Annas had at the top of the priority list to indict the pupils. More probable he wanted to get an admission that these men were being set up for progressive action. Jesus overlooked the matter.

So far as his educating was concerned, he denied having given mystery direction that may be interpreted as plotting against the experts. He had educated transparently, out in the open places, for example, the synagogue and sanctuary. His educating was not subversive.

21. Why askest thou me? Jesus suggested that the method was unlawful. There were no witnesses. He was being made to embroil himself by his declaration.

22. On of the going to officers (others were in the patio) thought the appropriate response impudent and struck Jesus to make him more accommodating in his state of mind toward the devout cleric.

23-24. At the point when Christ called attention to the treachery included, neither the officer nor Annas could make a barrier of the methodology. There was nothing to do except for to send the hostage to Caiaphas (the AV mistakenly proposes that he had been beforehand sent).

25-27. The story comes back to Peter. While Christ was denying the implications leveled against him - and fairly thus, Peter was denying his Lord wickedly. The two inquiries tended to Peter were very unique. The first was speculative, as if anticipating that him should deny that he had a connection to Jesus; while the second bound him, the very type of the question accepting his blame.

He was presently perceived as the person who had employed the sword in the garden. The crowing of the rooster helped Peter to remember the Lord's expectation (13:38) and conveyed home to him his wrongdoing of dissent. 'Chicken crowing' was the name of the third of the four watches into which the night was partitioned.

The Ordeal Before Pilate
(18:28 -19:16)

28. Nothing is said in regards to what occurred in the place of Caiaphas. The presumption is that the perusers are familiar with the Synoptic convention of the evening considerations and the formal declaration of the gathering touched base at in the morning.

The lobby of judgment (the home office of the senator). That they may eat the passover. The Jewish pioneers, to be ritualistically spotless, couldn't enter an agnostic's quarters. They were more worried with custom cleanness than with the execution of equity. They were determined to inflict some damage!

29-30. The Sanhedrin had not readied a formal prosecution against Jesus to submit to Pilate. They anticipated that the representative would believe them that this man was an evildoer, i.e., a practitioner of insidiousness. The appropriate response was nervy. Pilate was despised by the Jews.

31. Judge him as per you law. Pilate was fulfilled that the very unclearness off the announcement by the Jewish pioneers showed

that the case was not one he expected to listen (cf. Acts 18:14). It is not legal for us to execute any man.

Every one of the Jews needed was a decision of death, the specialist of the representative to cover their own ruling against Jesus. The taking endlessly of the privilege to dispense capital punishment made the Jews acknowledge they were a subject people. This had special cases, as on account of a man, even a Roman, who transgressed the hindrance that isolated the Court of the Gentiles from the internal segment of the sanctuary zone.

Stephen's demise appears to disregard John's announcement, however it might have been founded on the learning of the Jews that the representative would not meddle all things considered.

32. Jesus had anticipated that he would pass on by torturous killing, a Roman technique for discipline, while the Jews utilized stoning (cf. Matt. 20:19).

33. Pilate then took matters into his own hands, addressing Jesus inside the Praetorium. John appears to assume that his perusers knew the Synoptic record, which incorporated a

charge leveled by the Jews against Jesus such that he had announced himself ruler of the country.

Pilate was obliged to inspect this matter on the grounds of conceivable revoluntionary aim. Craftsmanship thou the King of the Jews? "Thou" is vehement, as if Pilate were amazed that the appearance and disposition of Jesus so minimal fitted the claim of sovereignty. The detainee appeared to be innocuous.

34. Before he could answer the question, Jesus had to know whether it originated from Pilate himself as a Roman authority or whether it was only passed on as a touch of prattle. Maybe the devout cleric had examined the case with Pilate when he requested Roman officers to help in catching Jesus.

35. Pilate, unwilling to be caught into a confirmation that he had anything to do with the circumstance, put the obligation on the Jews. Thine possess country. Pilate could barely have felt the tenderness recommended by his words (cf.1:11).

36. My kingdom is not of this world. "He doesn't state that this world is not the circle of His power, but rather that His power is not of

human beginning" (Hoskyns, 1940). He was not a danger to the Roman expert. There was no place for the utilization of drive in his kingdom.

37. Pilate was nonplused. Here was a man who had discussed his kingdom three circumstances in fast progression, yet he had none of the outward signs of majesty. Workmanship thou a ruler then? Pilate could scarcely trust that anybody would confuse the figure before him for a lord.

Thou sayest that I am a lord. Jesus was reluctant to avow that he was a lord, keeping in mind that Pilate misconstrue the way of his majesty, which he now clarified as far as truth. Christ had come to hold up under observer to it. Heareth my voice (cf. 10:3,16).

38. Pilate saw that Jesus had no sympathy toward governmental issues or issues of state and was far expelled from a warlike soul, thus he ended the meeting, saying rather contemptuously, it appears, What is truth? He was no scholar nor religionist, however a man of activity.

Fulfilled that the detainee was not unsafe to Rome, he declared this to the Jews outside. No blame. This refers to purity in this unique situation, however to blamelessness of any wrong doing the Jews had charged against him.

39. Detecting the persistence of the rulers in their craving to get a conviction, Pilate thought he saw an approach to get around them and maintain equity by discharging the detainee. It was a yearly custom at Passover time for the representative to satisfy the group by discharging one detainee whom they asked.

Pilate imagined that, since Jesus was exceptionally famous, the general population who had assembled at this point for their yearly demand would look for his discharge.

40. Again John presupposes an information of the Synoptic story by his reference to Barabbas. Thief. Scoundrel (cf. Acts 3:14).

CHAPTER
NINETEEN

The Ordeal Continumn
(19:1-16)

1-3. At Pilate's request the detainee was scourged. This was the representative's second catalyst, the prior endeavor to secure discharge having fizzled as a result of the inclination for Barabbas. Pilate thought the Jews may be fulfilled if Jesus were embarrassed and made to endure in this design.

The Lord had anticipated this treatment (Matt. 20:19). See Isaiah 53:5 too. A crown of thistles. This was joke with respect to the officers, in perspective of Jesus' affirmed majesty. Some have thought this crown was designed from the sharp prongs of the date palm, in this way interfacing it with the patriot any expectations of the Jews communicated by the waving of palms when Jesus entered Jerusalem.

Since the palm was a statement of Jewish trusts in freedom even in Maccabean days, this activity by the troopers would have been the cruel answer of Rome to the Jews in general. From the Biblical stance the thistles might be said to express the scourge of wrongdoing (Gen. 3:17,18), which God was bearing for the race. A purple robe. Regularly connected with sovereignty. Dressed accordingly, Jesus turned into a protest of game and mishandle by the officers.

4-5. Pilate ..... went forward once more. He proposed to set up the path for the appearing of Jesus by a vainglorious declaration. Observe, I deliver him to you. This was the soul of the joke of the fighters. He, the Roman senator, would show the person who was rumored to be a lord however now unquestionably couldn't be mistaken for a ruler.

See the man! It is indeterminate what Pilate intended to infer here. Some find in the circumstance a craving to make feel sorry for in the hearts of the Jews. Be that as it may, the setting proposes progressively the prospect of contempt. Man may amount to just "hopeless animal."

In any occasion, Pilate's words, I discover no blame in him, have a bizarre ring. In the event that the detainee was honest, why was flagellating directed?

6. The appropriate response of the central clerics was a reverberating refusal to be happy with discipline of this character, however

difficult and embarrassing. Execute, Crucify! Pilate's answer, Take ye him, puts accentuation on the ye. As it were, "If there is any killing to be done here, you should do it."

Pilate was separating himself from the Jews' longing, however not genuinely offering consent to them to execute Jesus.

This was the third time the representative proclaimed himself not able to discover any blame (aitia) in Jesus. The word is utilized here in the lawful feeling of a legitimate ground of grumbling.

7. Pilate was remaining on Roman law. The Jews put something else over against it. We have a law. Accentuation falls on the we. Our law requires the demise of the detainee, since he made himself the Son of God. The individual section out of sight is Leviticus 24:16. Jesus had been blamed for irreverence amid his service (John 5:18) and at its nearby (Mark 14:62-64).

8. The more anxious. Pilate's past dread had been because of the furious perseverance of Jesus' informers, who might not be denied. Maybe John is presupposing his perusers' information of the fantasy of Pilate's significant other (Matt. 27:19). The senator's new dread

was that he was managing one who in some sense was heavenly - a child of a divine being.

9. It started to appear to Pilate that this case had more to it than he had suspected at first. So he took the prisoner inside the Praetorium for another meeting. Whence craftsmanship thou? Not habitation but rather beginning and nature were in view. No answer. Pilate's profound inadequacy (cf. 18:38) made answer pointless.

10. The quiet of the detainee irritated the senator. Maybe he believed that by affirming his power and propelling the update that crucial held tight his decision, he could make Jesus talk.

11. The gadget was just somewhat effective. Jesus talked, however just to state to Pilate his impediments. Control. Expert. Christ may have been certifying the expansive truth of the awesome control over the state (Rom. 13:1 ff.), however the anxiety falls on the quick circumstance. Pilate was feeble to do other than do the will of God for this situation.

He that conveyed me. Any references to Judas is not really normal here. The more noteworthy sin, i.e., more noteworthy than that of Pilate. "The transgression of Caiaphas is more prominent in light of the fact that Pilate's power is from God; and it was the obligation of Caiaphas to know and educate and in addition do the will of God.

In any case, he, the official illustrative of Israel, the People of God, has had plan of action to this rapscallion, who holds certain expert from God, all together that power presented by God for the execution of equity might be utilized for the execution of foul play"

121. Accordingly of this verbal trade, Pilate attempted recharged endeavors to discharge his detainee, driven alike by dread of this weird individual before him and by the conviction that he was not deserving of death. The Jews, detecting new determination in the representative, utilized their coming full circle contention. Thou are not Caesar's companion. The supreme sovereign was Tiberius, to whom Pilate was capable.

Here was a danger to take the case to the majestic court. Caesar would not have looked daintily upon a circumstance in which one was known as ruler without Roman assent. He would have seen this as treachery and may well have accused Pilate of negligence to obligation.

Doubtlessly the senator expected that if a grievance were made with respect to his treatment of this case, different inconsistencies in his organization would become visible.

13. The ideal opportunity for choice had come. Pilate .... sat down in the judgment situate. He had now to render his decision. Because of the unearthings of Pere Vincent, the Pavement is currently more likely than not recognized as the vast cleared territory that was a part of the Castle of Antonia, at the northwest corner of the sanctuary zone. Gahhatha most likely signifies "raised ground."

14. It was the arrangement of the passover. "The hour of the twofold relinquish is moving close. It is early afternoon. The Passover sheep are being set up for give up, and the Lamb of God is in like manner sentenced to death" (Hoskyns, 1940).

View your King! Whatever moved Pilate to make this last introduction (most likely contempt for the Jews - such a lord for such a people!), it was fortunately used to draw from the lips of the Jews an entire renouncement of their Messianic trust - We have no ruler however Caesar.

In the event that dialect implies anything,

the very power of God over the country was revoked. Who was liable of sacrilege now?

16. Conveyed. The verb is the same as that in verse 11. The Jews were currently ready to see their will fulfilled. Jesus was to be executed (Crucified).

The Crucifixion And Burial
(19:17-42)

17. Bearing his cross. All the Synoptics express that Simon of Cyrene was constrained to shoulder the cross. John alone expresses that Jesus conveyed it. Luke's record accounts for both. Jesus began, however couldn't convey it the distance. Golgotha. Most likely named from its appearance; thus an adjusted slope. It Latin identical is Calvary (Luke 23:33). It more likely than not been outside the city (Heb. 13:12).

18. Jesus in the middle. His was the place of focal significance, even his demise.

19. His position is clarified by the title fastened over the leader of the executed. Matthew and Mark utilize the word aitia, which John utilizes three circumstances, in his record of the trial, in the feeling of "charge." Pilate found no aitia

in Jesus that justified his demise, yet now he let the world realize that here hung Israel's ruler, as if along these lines including the country in disobedience of Rome and meriting this cruel reproach.

20-22. The very attention given the title (three dialects) and also the suggestion behind it enraged the Jews, so that the central cleric asked for that the wording be transformed from a reality to a claim. This Pilate declined to do, demonstrating an endurance which forcefully appears differently in relation to his shortcoming amid the trial.

23-24. Four fighters participated in the torturous killing (Acts 12:4). These took as individual ruin the articles of clothing of Jesus, separating them among themselves. Shoes, crown, external article of clothing (himation), and support were likely distrubed, leaving the more significant coat or tunie (chiton) for the throwing of parts. It has been proposed that in John's eyes this consistent robe may have symbolized the symbolized the bringing together force of the demise of Christ as securing the one run. The officers unwittingly satisfied Scripture by their activities (Ps. 22:18).

25-27. Three ladies, all named Mary, took their station close to the cross, dismally examining the person who was so dear to them. The Greek content, be that as it may, is somewhat ideal to the specify of four, the mother's sister (Salome, the mother of John) being noted however left anonymous.

Assuming this is the case, these four possibly proposed to display a kind of differentiation to the Roman troopers. Thoughtful for his mom, Jesus gave her into the care of the "adored supporter." His own brethren were not devotees as of now.

The solidarity of the Church, which the Lord was bringing into being, was to be otherworldly as opposed to regular (cf. Matt. 12:50). His own (home). On the off chance that John had a living arrangement in Jerusalem, his colleague with the consecrated minister is all the more promptly clarified (18:16).

28. I thirst. The physical need of the endure attested itself, the main outward sign he allowed to escape his lips. All things being equal, he expressed a reality instead of voicing an interest.

30. The vinegar was sharp wine. It resuscitated Jesus' quality, empowering him

to state (with a noisy cry, as per alternate Gospels), it is done. A similar word (tetelestai) has as of now occured in verse 28, rendered "achieved." Emphasis here is not on the closure of the sufferings but rather on the fruition of the mission of recovery. Surrendered the phantom. Conveyed over his soul (to God).

31. The sabbath day. Just a brief span stayed before nightfall and the happening to one more day. Regardless of what the day, the Law required the expulsion of casualties from the cross upon the arrival of death (Deut. 21:22,33). To have neglected this law at Passover time would have been a particularly appalling infringement of the Sabbath.

The breaking of the legs was intended to rush demise.

33-34. The trooper, finding that demise had bamboozled him of the joy of breaking the legs of Jesus, drove his lance into the side of the Savior. Blood and water. This is a significant sound event in the period promptly after death.

35. John joins solitary significance to this occurrence, for he gravely bears record to it. The passing of the Savior implies a nurturing stream; blood for the purifying from wrongdoing

and water for the representation of the new life in the Spirit (cf. I John 5:6-8).

36-37. These components of the demise of Christ additionally served to satisfy Scripture (Ps. 34:20; Zech. 12:10).

38-40. In the hour of Jesus' passing two mystery devotees found a valor they had not had some time recently. Joseph picked up from Pilate authorization to bring down the body from the cross; then Nicodemus approached to give the flavors and cloth to setting up the body for internment. For more data on Joseph, see Mark 15:43.

41-42. The mausoleum had a place with Joseph (Matt. 27:60). Entombment arrangements were rushed on the grounds that the day was finding some conclusion. Luckily, the spot was close to the place of execution. More total arrangement of the body could be made after the Sabbath.

CHAPTER

TWENTY

The Resurrection Appearances
(20:1-31)

The Sabbath rest in Jerusalem is passed by peacefully. The collection of Christ lay in the midst of the stillness of the tomb. Be that as it may, the "must" of Matthew 16:21 incorporates revival and in addition enduring and demise. The preeminent trial of the cases of Jesus of Nazareth was within reach.

1. The principal day of the week. The day after the Sabbath, or the third day from Christ's execution, as indicated by the typical Jewish technique for comprehensive retribution. Jesus' revival on this day decided the Christian day of love (Acts 20:7). Mary Magdalene. It was notable that few ladies came ahead of schedule to the tomb, Mary alone.

The nearness of others is accepted in the "we know not" of verse 2. It was the motivation behind the ladies to bless the assemblage of Jesus all the more for all time (Mark 16:1). The stone taken away. With the stone set up, Mary would have had the issue of accessing the tomb; with the stone expelled, she had an issue of another kind. To her mind, the circumstance had intensified.

2. Mary thought about the main followers - Simon Peter and the "cherished devotee' - and hurried to take the word to them. It is of intrigue that in Mary's eyes Peter, in spite of his dissent, was still the recognized pioneer of the gathering. John, to a degree in charge of Peter's disappointment (18:16), had been trying to solace him. Mary's report of the opened tomb recommended to the two educates a similar dread that had grasped her heart - somebody had taken the body.

3-4. Concern created the two followers to break into a run, leaving Mary to come at her own particular step. A similar concern drove John to sprint in front of Peter, however the two had begun together. John may have been the more young.

5. Stooping down. The musing is best spoken to by our oath "peer." Restrained by wonderment and meekness, John took in the inside of the tomb, however did not enter.

6-7. With his trademark strength, Peter did not delay at the passage to look, but rather went in, and was in this manner ready to see more obviously than John the aura of the grave garments. He saw that they were not all in a pile, but rather that the headpiece was flawlessly wrapped and kept in a place without anyone else's input.

On the off chance that the body had been evacuated, it was odd that the material fabrics were abandoned, and considerably more interesting that the napkin was so painstakingly organized. Wrapped together. This verb is utilized of the demonstration of winding grave garments about the group of Jesus before the entombment (Matt. 27:59; Luke 23:53).

It might connote that the head went through the napkin, abandoning it in its round shape, or that Jesus purposely collapsed it up before leaving the tomb.

8. Encouraged by Peter's passageway, John went along with him inside, took in the scene, and trusted that the Lord had risen. This is not said of Peter.

9. The pupils had not gotten guideline from Christ relating his restoration to the OT Scriptures (Luke 24:46). They had Jesus' expectation of revival yet did not comprehend this truly (Mark 9:10).

10. Their own home. The expression is truly, to themselves, implying that they came back

to their own quarters and to their own kin. Mary (cf. 19:27) would along these lines have scholarly of the void tomb soon.

11. Mary Magdelene stayed at the spot, seeking after some intimation to the whereabouts of Jesus, battling with her twofold anguish over his passing and the vanishing of his holy shape. She stooped down (cf. v. 5).

12. She saw something the two followers had not seen - two heavenly attendants. Such was the experience of the other ladies likewise (Luke 24:22,23).

13. Conventionally a dream of heavenly attendants would have brought an excite, yet Mary was excessively overborne with melancholy, making it impossible to feel whatever other feeling. She dismissed before getting any hint from them that Jesus was risen (cf. Check 16:6).

14-15. She was similarly uninterested in another shape that lingered up before her as she dismissed into the garden. Her exclusive concern was to press her look for the body, and quite possibly this man was the nursery worker and might have expelled it.

16. Charged at hearing her name talked in

the well known voice of Jesus, she burst out, Rabboni (Master or Lord). Initially the shape implied my incredible one, yet the word had come to be utilized without possessive constrain.

It is not unduly shocking that Mary perceived the voice of Jesus when he talked her name however not when he initially scrutinized her. Indeed, even the well known can appear to be bizarre to us when we experience it out of the blue.

17. Touch me not. The Greek requires an alternate rendering: Stop sticking to me. Clearly Mary's first motivation, in her free for all of euphoria, was to get a handle on the consecrated shape. Jesus did not censure the other ladies for holding his feet (Matt. 28:9), for this was a demonstration of love; nor did he recoil from welcoming Thomas to touch him (John 20:27).

Yet, Mary should have been shown that the Lord was not with her on the premise of the former relationship. He was at that point celebrated. He had a place now with the great domain, despite the fact that he was eager to hesitate for an opportunity to meet with his companions.

I am not yet rose. The suggestion was that

Mary would have the capacity to touch Jesus in some sense after the Ascension, i.e., she would touch him by confidence in the favored existence of the Spirit.

The closeness of that new relationship is bore witness to by the way that he talked about his supporters as brethren (cf. the suspicion of this in Matt. 12:49). Indeed, even in the closeness of the new request, be that as it may, Christ held his own unique relationship to God the Father. My Father is the dialect of god; my God is the dialect of mankind.

18. The feeling of being helpful, of satisfying Jesus' charge to go to the pupils, diminished any sentiment hurt Mary may have encountered at the repel she had gotten. Her assignment is a smaller than expected of that given to the entire Church - to go and tell that Jesus has risen.

19. The pupils, having gotten the message from Mary, now had their first open door, as a gathering, to see Jesus in his risen state. It was the night of the restoration day. Inspired by a paranoid fear of the Jews. This was normal in perspective of their flight from the garden, Annas' request about them (18:19), and the desire made by Jesus' showing that in the event

that he endured, they ought to hope to do as such likewise (Matt. 16:24; John 15:20). The suggestion is plain that Jesus went through shut entryways. He had energy to dematerialize his body. Peace be unto you (cf. 14:27; 16:33).

20. The expression of peace had mitigated dread. Presently it was so as to set up personality. He indicated unto them his hands, and his side. As per Luke, considerably more realistic show was required keeping in mind the end goal to bring conviction (Luke 24:37-43). At that point were the followers happy (cf. 16:22).

21. The principal "peace" (v. 19) was to calm their hearts; the second was to set them up for a crisp articulation of their bonus (cf. 17:18). Nothing had been changed in the arrangement of the Master for them.

22. He inhaled on them. This reviews the formation of man (Gen. 2:7), as if to declare the new creation, coming about less from the implantation of the breath of God as from the gathering of the Holy Spirit (cf. 7:39). This need not preclude any connection to the Spirit in the times of prior discipleship any more than it discounts the Spirit's happening upon them at Pentecost. Here the Spirit was the important

gear for the undertaking that lay ahead, which is expressed next.

23. Christ offered specialist to the messengers and conceivably to others (cf. Luke 24:33 ff.) to excuse and to hold the wrongdoings of men. "Either.... the pupils must have unfailing knowledge into man's heart, (for example, in specific cases was conceded to a messenger, cf. Acts 5:3), or the reduction which they announce must be restrictively broadcasted.

Nobody can keep up the previous option. It takes after, then, that what our Lord here focuses on His devotees, to His Church, is the privilege legitimately to pronounce, in my name, that there is absolution for man's wrongdoing, and on what conditions the transgression will be excused" (Milligan and Moulton, 1898).

This scene includes the passing of Christ (his injuries exhibited), his restoration (announced by his living nearness), the resultant commission to go and demonstrate the veracity of him, the gear for this undertaking, and the message itself, focusing in absolution of sins.

24-25. John notes Thomas' nonattendance yet does not clarify it. Since Jesus did not censure Thomas on the score of his losing enthusiasm for his discipleship, it is shaky for us to do as such. He may have wanted to be distant from everyone else in his misery over the Savior's passing.

The report of the others concerning their meeting with Jesus underlined that they had seen the injured hands and side of the Lord. Thomas requested seeing these, as well as the real touching of them as the state of trusting that Jesus was alive from the dead.

26. After seven days, with conditions the same as some time recently, including the close entryways, Jesus came a moment time and with a similar welcome of Peace.

27. By his exceptionally dialect the Lord uncovered that he comprehended what Thomas had declared. In this way he more likely than not been alive when the questioning witness talked those words about the hands and the side.

28. His second thoughts totally evacuated. Thomas rose to a strong presentation of confidence in light of Jesus' test. My Lord and my God. He knew he was within the sight of divinity.

29. Since thou hast seen me. There is nothing to show that Thomas touched the Savior. Seeing

him had been sufficient. Be that as it may, shouldn't something be said about the hoards who might not have this chance of sight? A gift is articulated on such, who set out to make the wander of confidence (cf. I Peter 1:8).

The Purpose Of This Gospel
(20:30-31)

30-31. The signs which dab the account of John have peaked in the best of them all, the Resurrection. Keeping in mind that the peruser suspect something, the author hurries to note that the signs were numerous. Just a chosen few are incorporated into this book.

However it is the essayist's desire that these will empower the peruser to trust that Jesus is the Christ (the question of Jewish desire, in light of OT prescience, when that desire is not distorted by bogus perspectives of Messiahship) and the Son of God uncovering the Father by word and deed, coming full circle in compliance to the Father's will even unto passing.

Accept incorporates the thoughts of confidence's underlying demonstration and of advancing in confidence too. Life through (more truly, in) his name, i.e., in union with his own particular individual.

Since this appears a characteristic conclusion to the Gospel, a few researchers have presumed that the following section was included later, either by John himself or by another. In any case, there is nothing to request such a perspective of the end section.

It is loaded with suggestiveness in the matter of how the Lord's proceeding with nearness and power empower the Church to satisfy its service on the planet.

CHAPTER

TWENTY-ONE

Epilogue
(21:1-25)

1. The scene of the post-revival appearances shifts from Jerusalem to Galilee. The ocean of Tiberias - another term for the Sea of Galilee (cf. 6:1).

2. Together. This is represented, not on the premise of a typical occupation, but rather on that of their discipleship and of their involvement in observing Jesus become alive once again. Subside and John were to figure conspicuously in the occurrence going to be connected.

3. I go an angling. Subside couldn't stand latency. Seeing his pontoon and the waters of his cherished Galilee, and maybe the need of keeping body and soul together, directed his sudden declaration. It is risky to infer that Peter was backpedaling to angling as a perpetual occupation.

Undoubtedly, the infinitive of the verb "to fish" is current state, which may recommend supported activity. Be that as it may, this is balanced by the way that the verb "I go" proposes an endeavor as opposed to a profession. Promote, the simultaneousness of alternate supporters makes it clear that they comprehended Peter's motivation to be brief.

In perspective of the appearances of the Lord to them (cf. 20:21-23), it is unbelievable that they were returning to angling as an occupation. They don't found anything. This was fortunate, setting up the path for Christ's intercession.

4-5. Remaining on the shore, Jesus talked however was not perceived. Youngsters might be rendered fellows without doing brutality to the importance. Have ye any meat? The type of the question conveys the doubt that they didn't have any.

Meat. Savor eaten with bread, additionally utilized as a part of the feeling of fish. No. It harms an angler to concede that he has found nothing.

6. Thrown the net on the correct side. The position of the vessel continued as before, the angling rigging was the same, the men were the same, with a similar aptitude, however now their vacant nets turn out to be full, all on account of the expression of Christ (see John 15:5).

7. The marvel conveyed brisk attention to the "cherished supporter" that the outsider must be Jesus. It is the Lord. Diminish's mind more

likely than not flashed back to some other time on this same lake when at Jesus' oath he let down the net and gathered an awesome catch of fish (Luke 5:1-11).

Subside's energy to see Jesus in person proposes that he was not aware of being out of the will of God in going angling. Taken a toll. It would have been disgraceful to welcome the Lord without being completely attired.

8. Alternate devotees followed in the dinghy. Two hundred cubits. Around one hundred yards.

9. Jesus' adherents were going to be reminded that the person who gifts accomplishment in Christian work is additionally adequate for the day by day needs of his own. Angle. A solitary fish. Bread. A solitary roll. Jesus would make them suffice, as he had finished with the rolls and fishes for the huge number.

10. Bring of the fish which ye have now gotten. The intention was not to expand what was at that point gave. There is no sign that the fish were arranged and cooked and eaten. Christ needed the men to get the full excite of their catch.

Liberally he stated, "which ye have now

gotten," in spite of their weakness separated from himself.

11. The fish were tallied, which is standard. Their number essentially shows the enormity of the catch. In the event that there is any imagery associated with the unbroken net, it is such that the individuals who are won through Christ - guided administration to achieve the great strand.

12. Eat. The word is particularly reasonable for breakfast, however utilize here and there of different suppers. It was a serious event, with the pupils feeling a new feeling of stunningness within the sight of the Lord.

14. The third time. Two different appearances to the devotees as a gathering are described in the past part. The rest of this appearance concerns solely Peter and John, however the others benefitted from the educating.

15. This scene has now and again been called "The Restoration of Peter," however this might misdirect. Subside had as of now been reestablished in the feeling of getting pardoning (Luke 24:34).

In any case, the initiative of a failing supporter could scarcely have been acknowledged for the days ahead, either by Peter or his brethren, aside from Christ's unequivocal sign.

Lovest thou me? More imperative than affection for men is love for Christ. More than these. Some comprehend "these" to allude to the gear of angling. In the event that this were thus, Peter could have replied with no avoidance and without the utilization of an alternate word for adoration than Jesus utilized.

The very reality that Jesus examined Peter's adoration within the sight of his brethren proposes that the others were included. Diminish had gloated that he would stay steadfast regardless of the possibility that the others didn't (Mark 14:29). Encourage my sheep. Christ is unwilling to depend his little ones to one who does not love him.

16. The second round of question and answer brings a to some degree diverse commission in any event verbally. Sustain my sheep is truly, Shepherd (or tend) my sheep.

17. Diminish's pain here might be followed to two things. To begin with, the triple question may well have recommended his three-overlay dissent. Second, Jesus surrendered his oath for adoration (agapao) and utilized the one Peter

utilized (phileo), a word demonstrative of warm love however maybe thought to be substandard compared to the next.

This qualification is blunted, notwithstanding, by the way that somewhere else in John the second word is utilized as a part of a high sense (e.g., 5:20). My sheep (cf. 10:14,27). They are valuable to the Lord; he gave his life for them. Dwindle required love to expect the peaceful office.

18. The acknowledgment of this commission was to demonstrate exorbitant. Early days in Peter's life were seasons of flexibility. One day this flexibility would be pulled back, yet just when Peter was old. The prescience guaranteed him of years of administration.

Extend forward thy hands. Appropriate dialect for execution. Early church custom backings this way of death for Peter.

19. By what (kind of) death. He would be regarded by agony demise in an indistinguishable way from the Lord.

"Glorify" has been utilized of the passing of Jesus likewise (12:23). Tail me. This prompted to a physical development, yet much is inferred (cf. 13:36). Diminish was being summoned to an undeviating, unwavering stroll, to set his face like stone, even as Jesus had done in perspective of the moving toward cross.

20. John took after additionally, without a welcome. Diminish saw it and remarked on it.

21. Being a companion of John, Peter was interested in the matter of what future the Lord had in view for this man.

22. The appropriate response of Jesus had one reason, to censure Peter for being occupied over John's future. It was sufficient for him to be worried about doing God's will in his own life. This reproach is proposed by the insistent thou, which is missing from verse 19.

23. Jesus' words, in any case, were promptly misinterpreted as a confirmation that John would live on until the Lord's arrival. The "if" was effectively overlooked. John himself amends this false impression.

24. This. A reference to that devotee in verse 23, i.e., John. Testifieth. This may indicate John's oral declaration of the things contained in the Gospel, in refinement from the way that he likewise thought of them.

We know. The personality of these people who here add their observer to the veracity of

John is obscure. Likely they were men related with John in Ephesus, perhaps senior citizens of the congregation.

25. The contemplation is an expansion of what has as of now been expressed in 20:30. I assume. This is ungainly after the plural we are aware of the past verse. Some believe John's secretary allowed himself this end word.

Again we are reminded that our Gospel records are not proposed to be full records of the action of our Lord in the times of his tissue.

BIBLIOGRAPHY

Allbright, W. F. (1961) The Archaeology Of Palestine. Reprint Edition. Gretna, (New Orleans) LA.: Pelican Publishing Company

Barth, K. (1958) Dogmatics In Outline. New York, NY.: Harper & Brothers Bernard, T. D. (1892, 2012) The Central Teaching Of Jesus Christ. New York, NY.: Macmillan & Company, Forgotten Books

Bonhoeffer, D. (1967) The Cost Of Discipleship. 2nd Edition. New York, NY.: Macmillian

Bonhoeffer, D. (1967) Letters And Papers From Prison. Revised & Enlarged Edition By Eberhard Bethge. New York, NY.: Macmillian

Brown, R. E. (1970) The Gospel According To John. 2 Vols. New York, NY,: Anchor Bible Series. Doubleday

Calvin, J. (1949) Commentary On The Holy Gospel Of Jesus Christ According To John.

2 Vols. Grand Rapids, MI.: William B. Eerdmans

Daube, D. (1994) The New Testament And Rabbinic Judism. Hendrickson Publishers

Dodd, C. H. (1953) The Interpretation Of The Fourth Gospel. New York, NY.: Cambridge University Press

Hoskyns, E. C. (1940) The Fourth Gospel. Edited By F. N. Davey. London, Eng.: Faber And Faber, LTD

Lightfoot, R. H. (1956) St. John's Gospel And Commentary. Edited By C. F. Evans. New York, NY.: Oxford University Press

Milik, J. T. (1959) Ten Years Of Discovery In The Wilderness Of Judea. Naperville, Ill.: Alec R. Allenson

Milligan, W. And Moulton, W. F. (1898) Commentary On The Gospel Of St. John. Edinburgh: T&T Clark

Palmer, E. (1978) The Intimate Gospel: Studies In John. Waco, TX.: Word Books Publisher

Pascal, B. (1941) Pensees. Translated by W. F. Trotter. New York, NY.: Random House

Temple, W. (1950) Readings In St. John's Gospel. London: Macmillian & Company

The Wycliff Bible Commentary (1968) Chicago, Ill.: The Moody Bible Institute Of Chicago

ABOUT THE AUTHOR

The Reverend Dr. John Thomas Wylie is one who has dedicated his life to the work of God's Service, the service of others; and being a powerful witness for the Gospel of Our Lord and Savior Jesus Christ. Dr. Wylie was called into the Gospel Ministry June 1979, whereby in that same year he entered The American Baptist College of the American Baptist Theological Seminary, Nashville, Tennessee.

As a young Seminarian, he read every book available to him that would help him better his understanding of God as well as God's plan of Salvation and the Christian Faith. He made a commitment as a promising student that he would inspire others as God inspires him. He understood early in his ministry that we live in times where people question not only who God is; but whether miracles are real, whether or not man can make a change, and who the enemy is or if the enemy truly exists.

Dr. Wylie carried out his commitment to God, which has been one of excellence which led to his earning his Bachelors of Arts in Bible/

Theology/Pastoral Studies. Faithful and obedient to the call of God, he continued to matriculate in his studies earning his Masters of Ministry from Emmanuel Bible College, Nashville, Tennessee & Emmanuel Bible College, Rossville, Georgia. Still, inspired to please the Lord and do that which is well – pleasing in the Lord's sight, Dr. Wylie recently on March 2006, completed his Masters of Education degree with a concentration in Instructional Technology earned at The American Intercontinental University, Holloman Estates, Illinois. Dr. Wylie also previous to this, earned his Education Specialist Degree from Jones International University, Centennial, Colorado and his Doctorate of Theology from The Holy Trinity College and Seminary, St. Petersburg, Florida.

Dr. Wylie has served in the capacity of pastor at two congregations in Middle Tennessee and Southern Tennessee, as well as served as an Evangelistic Preacher, Teacher, Chaplain, Christian Educator, and finally a published author, writer of many great inspirational Christian Publications such as his first publication: ***"Only One God: Who Is He?" – published August***

2002 via formally 1ˢᵗ books library (which is now AuthorHouse Book Publishers located in Bloomington, Indiana & Milton Keynes, United Kingdom) which caught the attention of **The Atlanta Journal Constitution Newspaper.**

Finally, Dr. Wylie's present publication in a series, "A Commentary On The Gospel Of John," by a God-fearing man who is not only an exceptional, a prolific writer or inspiring himself; but allows God to lead him. Dr. Wylie is one of whom many of his peers think very highly of and is well sought after by his peers.

ABOUT THE BOOK

Dr. John Thomas Wylie shows the reason for this book in the presentation, and states it is obvious in John 20:31. John wrote to demonstrate that Jesus was the Christ, the guaranteed (promised) Messiah (for the Jews), and the Son of God (for the Gentiles), and to lead adherents into an existence of celestial fellowship with Him. The Key word is "Trust" (Believe) We discover this word ninety-eight times in this book.

The subject of John's Gospel is the God of Jesus Christ. More here than anyplace else His awesome Sonship is put forward. In this Gospel we are demonstrated that the Babe of Bethlehem was none other than the "Only Begotten of the Father." There are confirmations and verifications given without number. Albeit all things were made by him, despite the fact that in him was life, yet He was made flesh, and dwelth among us. No man could see God; subsequently, Christ came to declare Him.

The Reverend Dr. John Thomas Wylie

Printed in the United States
By Bookmasters